Behavioral Approaches to Public Administration

ROBERT PRESTHUS

Behavioral Approaches
to
Public Administration

UNIVERSITY OF ALABAMA PRESS

University, Alabama

Second Printing 1972

COPYRIGHT © 1965 BY
University of Alabama Press, University, Alabama
Library of Congress Catalog Card Number 64–66422
Manufactured in the United States of America

To the memory of

Thorstein Veblen

Contents

List of Tables

Acknowledgments

IT IS A PLEASURE TO THANK ROBERT HIGH-saw, Chairman of the Department of Political Science, University of Alabama, for his warm hospitality and wise counsel during the time these lectures were given. I am equally indebted to Coleman Ransone, Jr., Educational Director of the Southern Regional Training Program, for his kindness and administrative care. I want also to thank the political science faculty, and particularly Walter Bennett, the SRTP Fellows, and other members of the University for their cordial reception and, not least, for their critical interest in the behavioral approach. Because the research in community power structure and organizational effectiveness reported in these lectures was done in close collaboration with Vaughn Blankenship, I wish to make clear my obligation to him. I owe much to Oxford University Press for its kind permission to include in this volume extensive excerpts from *Men at the Top: A Study in Community Power* (1964). Finally, I want to thank the directors of British European Airways and British Industrials, Ltd., for allowing me to work with their executives in London during 1963-64.

ROBERT PRESTHUS

December, 1964
Ithaca, N. Y.

Preface

IN 1964 THE DEPARTMENT OF POLITICAL
Science at the University of Alabama asked me to give
the annual Southern Regional Training Program lectures
in public administration. This invitation was particularly
gratifying as an indication of the growing recognition of
behavioral contributions to the field. In these lectures, I
have tried to suggest the utility of behavioral theory and
research by examples from my own work during the past
five years. Both losses and gains have been reported. Some
of my theoretical assumptions about the relationship between authority and behavior in big organizations failed
to meet the empirical test. Certainly, the assumed relation between deference to authority and mobility did not
appear.

On the other hand, the suggestive hypothesis that some
of the properties commonly identified as " authoritarian "
are associated with mobility survived. Obviously, a great
deal of work must be done in many kinds of organizations
before this relationship can be generalized. Nevertheless,
it is clear that further research is worthwhile. Significant
differences were found between American and British
executives regarding their conceptions of work and authority. Americans in private organizations seem more
likely to accept somewhat larger amounts of organizational
influence as being legitimate. They are also likely to be
much more conservative politically. Such variations seem
to be the result of deep-seated cultural differences between

the two societies, rather than the result of specific organizational influences.

One useful theoretical perspective is the combined use of power structure analysis and support theory to test the effectiveness of an organization. Such an approach seems applicable to most organizations in most social systems. Even relatively undeveloped societies possess the elements of class stratification, power disequilibria, and functional differentiation that permit analysis of the extent to which a given organization enjoys the support of those who hold favored positions in the existing power structure.

But such theoretical perspectives are no more significant than the fact that behavioral methods can open new research possibilities for our field. Obviously, such methods have been used for a long time in public administration, but the behavioral approach has never been the dominant research thrust in the field. Today, the development of new computer techniques and the increasing acceptance of behavioralism in social science make new departures much easier. We can handle vastly greater aggregates of data, and such once-complicated instruments as factor analysis have become simple. Behavioralism's interdisciplinary character remains a problem, but there is some evidence that the best alternative is to achieve a synthesis in one man's head, rather than to attempt the frustrating task of bringing together men from various disciplines. Behavioral research is no doubt expensive, but this is a rich society. Certainly, for those of us in the universities, its broad scope and its concern with theoretically-guided research can bring a new intellectual excitement to the field.

R. P.

Behavioral Approaches to Public Administration

1

Behavioralism as Mood and Method

IT SEEMS WELL TO BEGIN BY DEFINING BE-
havioralism so that we can have a roughly common agreement about its meaning. Like many terms, behavioralism
means different things to different people, but for the
moment, let me indicate what it means to me. Behavioralism is both a method and a point of view. My own belief
is that a certain methodological commitment is its major
differentiating characteristic. Certainly, behavioralists are
often concerned with traditional aspects of political science, including participation, political attitudes, public
opinion, and so on. Among traditional fields, perhaps only
political philosophy has been somewhat neglected. And
even here normative questions about elitism and pluralism
have inspired considerable behavioral research, as seen in
the fields of community power structure and political
values.

In political science, at least, behavioralism probably began as a protest against older historical, normative, essentially descriptive *kinds* of analysis, rather than against their
substance. Many political scientists felt that the discipline

was concerned too much with the form and the formal mechanics of government and politics. They objected to its emphasis upon highly normative questions; to its claims that certain truths and questions were permanently valid and relevant; and to its methods, which were usually introspective and deductive. In the field of constitutional law, for example, scholars like Herman Pritchett and Glendon Schubert applied the techniques of factor analysis and scaling to the decisions of Supreme Court justices in an attempt to get at any " major inarticulate premises " which might increase our knowledge of judicial behavior.[1] Students of community power structure have similarly tried to determine more precisely the conditions under which time-honored pluralist assumptions about political behavior are valid.

It is thus tempting to say that behavioralism is essentially the scientific study of human behavior. It may be regarded as a discrete way of selecting certain kinds of evidence with the explicit assumption that they provide more valid indicators of reality than other kinds of evidence obtained in other ways. This orientation, which usually implies the use of survey research, rests on the belief that some areas of political life lend themselves more readily than others to systematic analysis. This, in turn, suggests why behavioralism must also be regarded as a point of view or an approach.

Still, it would be wrong to treat behavioralism mainly as a protest against traditional methods and knowledge. At the moment, let me say only that a behavioralism that ignores historical political theory is apt to be sterile. The most significant research has often been concerned with testing one or another of the great normative issues with which political theory has concerned itself. Some observers insist that values cannot be studied scientifically, but behavioral research on elitism, pluralism, electoral and judicial behavior, political tolerance, alienation, and authoritarianism touches upon the most vital political questions. Aristotle, Rousseau, Voltaire, Locke, Madison, Marx, Calhoun, Veblen, and others asked such questions and to some extent our intellectual task is to make them operational, and also to answer them in the context of our own time.

One of behavioralism's basic characteristics is the acceptance of logical positivism as an epistemological system. Facts, publicly verifiable and sensually perceived, are regarded as the only valid basis of truth or reality. Values are seen differently as normative preferences whose validity is not subject to scientific proof. Behavioralism is properly identified with empiricism, by which I mean a temperamental and methodological affinity for aggregate factual data and field research. This temperamental aspect is worth mentioning because it seems that (as with about eighty per cent of political party affiliations) scholars have an inherent preference for either the behavioral or the nonbehavioral approach. Personally, for example, I happen to feel more secure when working with large aggregates of fairly specific, " hard " data. Since the reduction of anxiety is highly reinforcing, perhaps we may conclude tentatively that behavioralists are more anxious than other men. At the same time, I like to feel that my own research is concerned with theoretically and normatively significant questions, such as the individual's fate in large organizations and the structure of political leadership in American communities. Survey research, which is often regarded as the hallmark of behavioralism, is just too difficult an undertaking to be wasted on trivial questions,

Unfortunately, there is some evidence that behavioralism's scientific ethic may lead to "barefoot empiricism," to an atheoretical enchantment with facts at the expense of significance. Computer technology, it seems, has aggravated this tendency by making it much easier for the researcher to run his data through blindly, as it were, in an effort to find meaningful associations. In a way, however, this danger is exaggerated, if only because the researcher must have had, explicitly or otherwise, certain initial theoretical assumptions that determined the kinds of questions he asked. Once this commitment is made, it becomes difficult to put the data into a new perspective. One often sees this intrinsic difficulty in the results of so-called "secondary analysis," where data initially gathered within one theoretical context are strong-armed into another in an effort to use the data without the initial theory. But despite the fact that behavioral research is sometimes atheoretical, and despite the fact that some survey research experts can apparently produce useful relationships using *post hoc* interpretations, I think most behavioralists have learned that their research must be guided from the design stage by explicit theoretical constructs. This consciousness has been quite well manifested in recent community structure research, some of which will be discussed later to illustrate the general remarks being made here.

In discussing behavioralism one should note that it is a fairly recent phenomenon, certainly not over a century old. Indeed, the great strides have been made during this century, and it is fascinating, as Robert Merton notes, that about ninety per cent of the behavioral scientists who have ever lived are alive today. When we add them up (as a good behavioralist inevitably will) we find roughly some

45,000 scholars working in the four disciplines usually categorized as social or behavioral: anthropology, political science, psychology, and sociology. About half of these men are armed with a doctoral degree and are thus professionally equipped to do behavioral research. Some, of course, are more behavioral than others, with psychologists and sociologists at the high end of the continuum.

It seems useful to define behavioralism by its essential orientation, which is toward the systematic study of human behavior. Behavioralism often asks: How do individuals or groups *act*, as contrasted with institutionalized expectations and conventional assumptions about their behavior? Often, of course, individuals and groups conform nicely to such formal expectations. But we learn a great deal by the analysis of deviations from norms which characterize much of social behavior. All organizations exhibit a rough behavioral dichotomy between their public and their private faces. In sociological terms, they have both " manifest " and " latent " functions. Manifest or public functions are the official, conventional modes of behavior and mission which partially motivate an organization and legitimate its existence. Yet, along with these honorific values come latent private values, including the drive for power, security, and survival. Behavioral research and theory are often concerned with the latent facet of analysis.

In this sense behavioralism is revolutionary. It often challenges the Establishment and the ceremonial paraphernalia that sustain it. In showing the " functional " role of official myths, it tends to weaken them somewhat. I have little doubt, for example, that the restrained enthusiasm for behavioral science in business schools is based in part upon its awkward tendency to ask embarrassing normative questions. Computer technology, the current rage, seems much less likely to ask whether the emperor is really clothed.

This essentially skeptical role is not always productive, since most of us would agree that certain divine myths are necessary to hold society together. Indeed, when one looks at the endless variations of ethnicity, religion, and values in American society, he must wonder less that it doesn't run smoothly, than that it runs at all. Nevertheless, if we give a high priority to the search for knowledge, we may decide that our function is not, as Harry Truman had it, " to pass on the political myths to the young," but to play the iconoclastic role demanded by scientific progress.

Behavioral science's efforts to be methodologically rigorous provide another differentiating aspect: an explicit self-consciousness about the meaning of language and the criteria of verification, the use of consistent categories and the systematic collection of data are its hallmarks. Such rigor, in truth, is an impossible task, given the complexity and untidiness of the real world. Nonetheless, behavioralism is marked by a disciplined effort to be as systematic as possible, as I hope to show when I consider specific examples of research.

The fact is that dealing with facts through survey research makes one terribly aware of the difficulty of generalization. Behavioral research is a humbling experience. One learns with varying degrees of frustration that men are not consistent, that their attitudes are usually a mixture of liberal and conservative: that, for example, working-class people are usually *economically* liberal, i. e., they prefer more government intervention in the economy than upper-class citizens, but conservative insofar as *political* liberties are concerned. In two New York state communities we found about fifty per cent of working-class respondents unwilling to allow an atheist or a socialist to make a public speech on Main Street. Yet, only twenty per cent would agree that a "government that governed least governed best."

Perhaps such inconsistency explains why the behavioralist stresses the *tentative* and *cumulative* nature of his research and of knowledge generally. Ultimately, he says, we hope to be able to predict behavior under given conditions, but this will require further development of principles of individual behavior using similar categories and procedures, which will, in turn, require replication by scholars in the future. As Max Weber says, "Every scientific 'fulfillment' raises new questions; it *asks* to be surpassed and outdated . . . it is our common fate and, more, our common goal." [2]

Behavioralism's scientific thrust raises the question of its relationship to the psychological school called behaviorism. Behaviorism, of course, was the system founded by John B. Watson just before World War I, essentially as a protest against subjective psychology which used rationalism as its method and was primarily concerned with mental processes such as consciousness, will, and so-called affective elements. Impressed by the strides being taken in contemporary natural science, behaviorists insisted that psychology too should use the experimental method and deal exclusively with *behavior* which could be observed, analyzed, and classified. Laboratory study of animal behavior and the use of the stimulus-response mechanism became hallmarks of the new field. Prediction, the goal and test of all science, was achieved in experiments which showed that certain stimuli would typically produce certain responses. Pavlov's famous work on the conditioned response illustrates both the method of behaviorists and their ability (given certain conditions) to shape animal behavior. Behaviorism is closely allied with physiology and makes no analytical distinction between external and internal aspects of behavior. The overt response of Pavlov's dogs and growling of one's stomach when hunger occurs are regarded as being equally amenable to observation and measurement.

Like all systems, behaviorism has been modified in the light of experience. Psychology is less impressed today with the sharp Watsonian dichotomy between subjective and objective states, and many subjective elements such as perception and meaning are being investigated by rigorous methods. In general, behaviorism's early lack of sophistication has been overcome. For example, it is now recognized that " facts " are not really hard, objective realities, but are subject to perceptual sets and error. While some of behaviorism's enchantment with facts and method remains, as suggested by the highly focused work of experimental psychologists, the main drift is toward broader conceptions of both substance and method.

Behavioralism is similar to Watsonian behaviorism. Both are a protest against earlier, speculative systems; both stress observation and measurement of objective, sensually perceivable activity; and both have in mind the objective of prediction. Differences between the two systems are probably found less in method than in the material with which they are mainly concerned. Perhaps we may say that the behavioral approach uses many of the methods and assumptions of the earlier school, but it often uses them to analyze some of those internal states of conscious-ness—for example, political values and personality struc-ture—which behaviorism once rejected as unfit subjects for systematic research.

A suggestive difference between behavioralism and more traditional approaches is again seen in their concept and use of language. Despite his linguistic facility and nice literary sense which makes typical behavioral writing appear flat and simple, the traditional scholar has prob-ably been less interested in the limitations of language as an instrument of precise communication. He has not al-ways been concerned with whether a concept has a definite empirical referent or whether there is a difference between a word as a symbol and the object it represents.

Instead, I think one can fairly say that language is some-times looked upon as having both analytic and ornamental functions. In contemporary political writing one finds that synonyms are sometimes used to sustain literary in-terest, even though their meanings are inevitably some-what different.[8] We see writing that is highly polished, urbane, and erudite, but which may be almost reckless when analyzed from a systematic standpoint. I must say, parenthetically, that I was sharply impressed by these dif-ferences during my recent experience in England, where the classical allusion and the nicely-turned phrase are highly valued in writing and sometimes used at the ex-pense of careful analysis.

This literary thrust may be contrasted with behavioral writing which tends, in S. I. Hayakawa's term, to be more of a *report* form. Rich, evocative terms are avoided and the prose is often flat and descriptive. Let me cite three examples from works on philosophy, organizations, and small groups. The first of these examples was written by a classical philosopher, the second by a consultant-journalist-teacher, and the third is the contribution of an eminent behavioralist.

> Reason is substance, as well as infinite power, its own infinite material underlying all the natural and spiritual life; as also the infinite form, that which sets the material in motion. Reason is the substance from which all things derive their being.[4]

> No society can function as a society unless it gives the individual member social status and function, and unless the decisive social power is legitimate power. The former establishes the basic frame of social life: the purpose and meaning of society. The latter shapes the space within the frame: it makes society concrete and creates its institutions. If the individual is not given social status and function, there can be no society but only a mass of social atoms flying through space without aim or purpose.[5]

> Just as several variables are included under the concept of activity, so several are included under interaction. We can study the *frequency* of interaction: the number of times a day or a year one man interacts with another or the members of a group interact with each other. We can measure the ratio between the amount of time one man is active, for instance, talking, and the *duration* of his interlocutor's activity. Or we can study the *order* of interaction: Who originates action? Where does a chain of interaction start and where does it go?[6]

Since intellectual currents usually tend to reflect national experiences and character, it seems useful to note that whereas the traditional approach is essentially European in origin, behavioralism seems peculiarly American.

Not that we may claim to have invented behavioral science.[7] This achievement probably belongs to European psychologists and sociologists, including Freud, Pavlov, Galton, Binet, Weber, Durkheim, Simmel, Pareto, and Hobhouse. But the subsequent development of behavioral science has been overwhelmingly American. The important point is that the explicit method and the honoring of facts which characterize it are nicely suited to the pragmatic thrust in the American character. The inquiring mind, the acceptance of change, and the appeal to evidence seem relatively more common in the United States than in Western Europe.* Of course the availability and commitment of resources is a vital corollary. In the United States there are over 20,000 psychologists, 8,000 political scientists, and a similar number of sociologists and anthropologists. The rich support for research and the intensive work of these highly-trained men, who far outnumber their colleagues in Western Europe, also explain why behavioral science has flouished in America.

Speaking of support for social research, it is useful to look at a few figures. In May, 1964, the *American Behavioral Scientist* estimated that the total amount of federal funds spent for social science research is about $210 million per year. This figure, moreover, does not include classified research projects which, they say, might increase the amount by half. About two-thirds of the total is devoted to " in-house " research and the remainder to " outside " (mainly university) research and to what have been called " captive " private research organizations such as RAND,

---

* It is significant that one of the most neglected areas in American research has been social change. Perhaps this is because the accommodation of change has rarely been a great problem in our young culture.

the Hudson Corporation, and the Research Analysis Corporation, all of which depend almost exclusively on the Defense Department. A related and somewhat neglected question is the over-all impact of federally-sponsored research on the universities, some of which now receive as much as fifty per cent of their total annual revenues in such funds.[8] The proportion allocated to social research is low, around ten to fifteen per cent. Regarding the country as a whole, about $15 billion a year (three per cent of gross national product) is spent on scientific research of all kinds. Of this vast sum, however, only three per cent is spent for social science research. Foundations have a better record, for some thirty per cent of their grants are for work in the social sciences.

These figures give us some idea of the magnitude of social science research, much of which is behavioral. Much of its growth has occurred during the past two decades. Roughly, we may say that the amount available has expanded some fifteen to twenty times since World War II. At least, this is the amount by which *all* U. S. research spending has increased, and we may assume that behavioral research has increased proportionately.

The Behavioral Approach

Having outlined broadly the scope of behavioral science, I would like to consider the behavioral approach somewhat more specifically. Sensual and mainly visual apprehension of social facts is the basic mode and material of behavioralism. In this context, inferences, abstractions, hearsay evidence, and the like, must be regarded as essentially different and less reliable bits of reality. Of course, there are still problems in linguistic representation of these facts and different interpretations of the same event. Yet, the public nature of behavioral philosophy forces us to try to develop a science of behavior by relying upon agreement reached by several observers—using roughly similar theoretical frameworks—about a given network of behavior. Such behavior must be directly and publicly observable. The common logic of behavioralism, as psychologist Ernest Hilgard says, is " that scientific disputes can be arbitrated by an appeal to objective facts—objective in the sense that the relationship can be reproduced or observed by other competent people who do not share the initial biases of the one who first calls attention to the fact." Confirmatory reports by several investigators thus become the first requisite of valid knowledge.

From this we immediately see why the wisdom of a single individual, of purely individual experience, can never provide the basis for a behavioral science of politics or administration. When we touch upon the problems of epistemology, meaning, and language inevitably raised by a sophisticated behavioralism, we also see why the world of unvarnished commonsense and experience is of only limited relevance.

The critical failure in rationalist thought is its essentially deductive orientation: conclusions are derived from given premises whose validity cannot be established. As Hans Reichenbach shows, the syllogism provides an example of this critical distinction between rationalist and empiricist assumptions.[9] " All men are mortal. Socrates was a man; therefore Socrates is mortal." Here, the conclusion is analytically implied by the premises; it does not add anything to them, but merely makes some part of their content more explicit. By contrast, consider the inference: "All crows so far observed were black; therefore all crows in the world are black." Here, the conclusion is not part of the premise, but refers to crows not yet observed and extends to them a property—blackness—of all observed crows. Although the truth of the proposition cannot be guaranteed, because a white crow might conceivably appear, we need such inferences if we want to establish a general truth, which must include a reference to unobserved things. Before science could proceed beyond its Greek legacy with its expectation of absolutely certain truth, it had to accept this inherent risk of error contained in all inductive inferences, and to adopt a probabilistic view of the universe.

Bacon, whose fame rests mainly on his recognition of the significance of inductive inferences for the development of empirical science, made the first attempt at an inductive logic in the *Novum Organum*, written about 1620. Within the next century Locke and Hume added greatly to the new empirical logic, which differed essentially from rationalism, and indeed went too far in denying that reason had any part to play in scientific work. This mistake was rectified by modern empiricists who recognized the essential difference between statements about the observed present and those about the unobservable future. Locke was especially significant in showing that perception is the source and the final test of knowledge. Experience, he insisted, is the pen which writes upon a blank mind: "Nothing is in the mind that was not previously in the senses." This was quite different from earlier rationalist assumptions.

Illustration of this difference may be seen in traditional

philosophic conceptions of the state. Although the practice is becoming less common, for long the state was conceptualized abstractly as an entity which had, as in the German idealist versions, an existence apart from and above its constituent parts. In a nice example of what Arthur Bentley called " spooks," the state was seen as some mystical, monistic being, superior both morally and juridically to its members and its voluntary associations. Pluralism, by the way, was initially conceived in France as a counterpoise to this view. But the important point is that the state was conceptualized less as a tangible, observable reality than as a " brooding omnipresence."

Against this kind of thinking, behavioralists insist that the concept of the state be redefined in order to make it subject to empirical investigation. They insist that unless, in positivist terms, one can perceive the state in some sensual and public way, one is dealing only with a concept unanchored in any finite reality. Behavioralists are not content to accept the dicta of legal philosophers, however learned, that they have a monopoly of insight regarding the true character of the state. Knowledge, in effect, must rest on something more than personal authority.

This suggests again the essential difference between traditional and behavioral approaches. Heavily influenced no doubt by the physical sciences, behavioralists try to make explicit their whole design and machinery of research. They ask that no generalization be made to rest upon the insight or authority of any given scholar. Instead, they ask for complete publicity as to the conceptions, values, and method by which knowledge has been obtained in order to make possible its replication by others. The critical role of insight, hunch, and perceptual facility is recognized, but these are not accepted as an adequate basis for scientific truth. Instead, in the behavioral view, the latter must receive the most incisive scrutiny and be proved according to the best criteria in the social science armamentarium.

This emphasis upon the extrapersonal quality of knowledge has at least one useful by-product: it takes the sting out of criticism by the assumption that knowledge is cumulative and at any given time necessarily unfinished. Critical analysis thus profits from a detachment that is not always apparent in traditional research, where generalizations tend sometimes to be viewed as the personal property of a scholar. Of course, this private property view of knowledge is not entirely attributable to any given method; it is perhaps equally the result of the human tendency (aggravated by the mass media's need for oversimplification) to personalize events. But the point remains: the public orientation of behavioral research encourages free and dispassionate criticism through its emphasis upon the accretive, tentative nature of knowledge.

Yet another quality of behavioralism is its emphasis upon group effort to solve a common problem. In part this is because its material is usually interdisciplinary and its method calls for several discrete skills. Perhaps more significant is the fact that the scale of its research is often beyond the capacity of a single worker. There is also the belief that several trained minds can probably bring more insight to the design and analysis of research. The critical need in behavioral research is always to place its findings within some theoretically significant framework, to use the data to illumine problems that are truly meaningful. And finally, the accretive view of knowledge is sympathetic to collective effort. " Scientific work is group work; the contributions of individual men to the solution of a problem may be smaller or larger, but will always be small compared to the amount of work invested in the problem by the group. There are great mathematicians, physicists, and biologists; but even the greatest among them would have been unable to do their work without the preparation by preceding generations or the help of their contemporaries . . . The social character of scientific work is the source of its strength; the limited power of the individual is supplemented by the resources of the group, the slips of the individual are corrected by his fellow workers, and the resultant of the contributions of many intelligent individuals is a sort of superpersonal group intelligence, which is able to find answers that a single individual could never find." [10]

Allied is the behavioral recognition that research should attempt to cut across time and space to achieve what Arthur Bentley called " durational knowledge." Here again, behavioralism is extrapersonal in its insistence that purely individual experience and knowledge are necessarily time-and-space bound. Cognition must occur within the linguistic and conceptual apparatus of one's own culture and time; hence, this limitation is always with us. Although ahistoricism is often characteristic of behavioral research, which typically cuts out a single slice of time, ideally, at least, behavioralism seeks continuity.

Durational knowledge can be built into behavioral research. Panel studies of electoral behavior are primitive steps in this direction. In community power structure research, one can select a panel of decisions covering periods of about a decade. Clearly, this practice engages many of the traditional difficulties of historical research, including the inability of respondents to recall accurately the facts of a past decision. On the other hand, documents of many kinds are available to provide the researcher with background data against which responses can be checked. Newspaper accounts of a significant community decision, minutes from official and voluntary committees, and reports of various kinds to higher governments and financial houses are among such sources. By comparing lists of participants in earlier and contemporary decisions, one discovers clues that reveal any changing bases of power in a community. For example, trends may appear which show political leaders challenging or even replacing economic leaders in a position of dominance.

One finds, too, that common sense explanations rather than secular changes in class or economic structure also help account for such variations. The advanced age of former leaders is often cited as a reasonable explanation of changes in configurations of local power. But even such a simple finding can open fruitful channels by further specification. Do these associations between age and declining power vary among different occupational, ethnic, and income groups? Do, for example, those who play essentially political roles tend (as a look at some of our Congressmen suggests) to retain their power longer than leaders with other bases of power? And does this phenomenon, in turn, vary in communities with differing ecological bases?

Such longitudinal analyses enable us to make statements that encompass at least a limited historical period. In so doing we can ease the ahistoricism that is to some extent a structural property of survey research, the typical (although not the only) method of behavioralism. Durational knowledge not only reveals the endless change and complexity of social systems, but also explains the somewhat irritating insistence of behavioralists that generalizations apply only under certain given conditions. This tendency is particularly common and frustrating in experimental psychology, probably the most behavioral of the social sciences.

It may be useful to mention one further point of tension between the behavioral and the traditional schools: the claim that behavioralists are not concerned with values. In its extreme form, this claim may include the charge that behavioralists have no personal values. Perhaps the main point here is that the behavioralist believes his attempts to study the values of others require detachment on his own part. Values, in this context, are merely objective data which can be analyzed in the same way as less volatile social phenomena. However, this attempt to remain detached professionally has nothing to do with the personal values held by the behavioralist *qua* citizen. He may be somewhat less certain of the validity of his normative preferences, but he holds to them as strongly as his traditionalist colleagues. Certainly, a professional and intellectual awareness of the analytical difference between statements of fact and statements of value, and between one's role as researcher and one's role as citizen, need not lead to moral nihilism.

Although the conflict about values has become less strident, another basis of tension between behavioralists and traditionalists remains active. This is the interdisciplinary problem. Even though many of us would admit that the compartmentalization of disciplines within social science reflects professional and organizational imperatives rather more than intellectual realities, compartmentalization partly explains the reluctance of some scholars to adopt a more behavioral, that is, interdisciplinary style. This ambivalence stems from the fact that the whole academic reward system is geared to the existing departmental system. One achieves professional status through a network of intradisciplinary relationships institutionalized in the various professional associations. An elaborate exchange structure of reciprocal patronage exists within each discipline, providing a nice behavioral study in which reference group theory is a useful analytical construct. The ground rules are such that the use of alien disciplinary concepts is professionally suspect. Such departures tend to be viewed as challenges to the revealed wisdom of the discipline; perhaps they suggest that it is not fully capable of analyzing its own field. They tend, moreover, to disturb long-established subject-matter boundaries within the universities, often worked out to insure an equitable distribution of the intellectual spoils. Such " rate-busting " behavior seems particularly characteristic of sociology, which has now gathered unto itself a fulsome intellectual domain, comprising the " sociology of " cosmos, that is, of war, peace, religion, culture, politics, work, and leisure. It is worth noting, parenthetically, that this expansion has been greatly eased by the versatility of survey research, which can be applied to almost all social phenomena.

Another more convincing reason for the reluctance of political scientists to adopt a behavioral approach is the large investment in time required to master the language, theory, and methods of one or two additional disciplines. Much of the theory and method that has proved useful in political and organizational analysis is sociological, and the " retooling " required before one can use it understandably evokes mixed feelings.

A striking difference between what I have called the traditional and the behavioral approach relates to the discrete roles played by the researcher in each, mainly because of the different conditions of research that characterize each approach. My own view is that the behavioralist's role is somewhat more difficult. He tends to deal more precisely with more explosive material. His focus is usually quite specific and intensive, which means that it becomes very difficult to mask criticism with studied imprecision or a highly abstract level of discourse. His research, moreover, is often both temporally and politically current. In engaging deeply-felt values, he often reveals the inevitable gap between the ideal and the real, between comfortable, ego-reinforcing explanations of behavior and the cool interpretations of an uncommitted observer. For these reasons his findings are almost sure to disenchant someone.

A related problem concerns the protection of respondents. If he is to receive co-operation and candid responses, the researcher must usually guarantee anonymity. And it is of course ethically proper that this be done. Unfortunately, it is not always possible to mask the identities of certain public figures. In my study of two communities which I called Edgewood and Riverview, for example, both mayors were in the upper reaches of the local power structure. Referring to them as Mayors King and O'Brian technically met our commitment, but it was really impossible to disguise them without distorting the entire analysis.

Such ethical tensions are probably inherent in all research, but they seem aggravated in the behavioral field. To carry out a study, the researcher must make several concessions. In addition to protecting his informants, he must sometimes let those concerned review the final manuscript and suggest changes before publication. Again, public relations may loom large in the perspectives of his own university, which has a legitimate (if sometimes overdrawn) interest in maintaining smooth relationships with outside interests.[11] Such constraints mean that the behavioralist often knows from the start that he will probably irritate, disappoint—if not infuriate—some of those with whom his research deals. His scientific ethos demands that he report the facts as fully and precisely as possible, yet various restrictions, as well as the personal attachments that often develop during an extended study, make such reporting difficult. I shall never forget the comment of Mayor O'Brian, who answered my initial request for his co-operation with the words, " Why yes, I'll be glad to talk with you because I feel sure you wouldn't want to hurt Riverview." Such a comment suggests why the end results of field research often include the disturbing feeling that one has been obliged to upset those who have made his research possible.

My own reluctant conclusion is that behavioral research is often controversial, and that the researcher must often offend someone. I submit that the traditional scholar is less likely to encounter this difficulty by the very nature of his inquiry. In political science, for example, research and writing are often normatively positive and historical, which tends to make controversy somewhat less likely. Pluralism, with its comforting conclusion that power is widely shared in our society, that every man enjoys considerable indirect influence in political decisions, provides an example of this orientation. Similarly, the scholar who writes about men and events in the past is unlikely to alienate anyone. Not only are the principals gone but time lends respectability to even the most confirmed rascal. Meanwhile, we all seem to share the satisfying illusion about unhappy past events that "such things might have happened in those days, but they don't happen any longer."

One last tension, which I have noticed particularly in my European work, involves status problems in survey research. One must frankly recognize that researchers themselves have status needs and that the relative status of researcher and respondent are significant elements in the interview process. To some extent, regardless of the prestige structure of the interview situation, the researcher finds himself in a position of dependence. He has, after all, asked the respondent for both his time and his opinions. In his efforts to gain rapport, he has made various concessions. Typically, the respondent is asked to set the time of the interview at his convenience. The researcher comes to his home or office. At any point, the respondent can refuse to co-operate with impunity. In effect, the respondent's vital role in the research is often made dramatically patent; the extent probably varies with the anxiety of the researcher.

The resulting dependency may prove difficult for the researcher. And here, of course, his own personality structure is important. He must be supple enough to assume his role wholeheartedly in order to avoid interpersonal strain between himself and the respondent. Recent findings about "acquiescence set," which show that lower-class respondents tend to give affirmative responses to affirmatively-stated items, in part because they defer to the " middle-class " status of the researcher, emphasize the importance of status factors in the interview situation.[12] My point here, however, is that there are many situations in which the researcher must assume a role of dependency. In societies where survey research is still exceptional, this problem may be aggravated because the respondent's definition of a professor does not usually include one who involves himself in dependency relations with people of varying status and prestige levels. The relatively higher status of professors in Europe compared with the United States is an example of the impact of culture upon research.

Such tensions may be eased by the use of a staff of hourly-paid interviewers who conduct the field research while the professor remains aloof from such mundane work. My own view, however, is that the costs are high in terms of the attending loss of " feel " for the data by those who must finally interpret and mould them into some theoretically significant whole. In sum, status incongruity is yet another tension of behavioral research that is less typically characteristic of traditional research.

2

Behavioral Research
in Community Power Structure

WE NOTED EARLIER THE INSISTENCE OF BE-
havioralists that concepts and terms be " operationalized,"
that they be linked with empirically observable, testable,
public phenomena. Take, for example, the concept of
power, which most of us agree is the essential stuff of
political science. This benchmark concept has remained
unsatisfactory precisely because it has remained too abstract and too rarely subjected to operationalization and
empirical test. Here we owe the Lynds, Warner, and
Hunter [1] a great debt for having inspired by their community studies a more systematic investigation of power,
its mechanics, and its bases. Upon their foundation, a
more sophisticated conceptualization of this vital element
in political behavior is beginning to be built.

Hunter has perhaps revealed more than his early colleagues about how he isolated power.[2] Essentially he used
what has been called the " reputational " method whereby
prominent figures in a community are simply asked to
designate men who have the capacity to " move things."
Power, in effect, was operationally defined as the capacity

to influence policy outcomes. It was not, however, to be measured in terms of empirical evidence of such influence. If observers *believed* that certain individuals had this capacity, they nominated them to the reputational list. In Atlanta, Hunter's initial list of some 160 men was refined to produce 40 leaders who reputedly formed the nucleus of power in the city. Despite vigorous (and occasionally unfair) criticism by some pluralists who perhaps forgot that knowledge proceeds incrementally and who may have been slightly disenchanted by his conclusion that power in Atlanta resembled the elitist model, Hunter's work remains significant. It has inspired a great deal of subsequent thought and research which has given us a more incisive conception of power. It seems ironic that whereas we tend to accept incrementalism in physical science and engineering—for example, no one is exercised over the fact that the Douglas DC-3 has been superseded by the Boeing 707—social science sometimes displays a more rigid view of intellectual priority and ownership.

For our purposes, however, it is necessary to emphasize that Hunter's reputational method does not entirely meet going criteria of verification. His method purports to identify those who have power, yet it does not in fact *demonstrate* that nomination to the reputational list is associated with the actual use of power. Men on the list may be well-known, rich, charming, skillful, and so on, but the mere possession of these qualities does not prove that they are in fact powerful. Some empirical test of their overt use of such resources seems to be required.

Hunter's findings also touched upon the major bases of power in American communities. He found that power rested mainly on social class, that high power was highly associated with upper-class status and economic affluence. This unexceptional conclusion inspired further research by observers who apparently doubted that such resources constitute critical bases of political power.[3]

The beginnings of such a test were provided by Robert Dahl's study of New Haven, in which participation and influence in three kinds of decisions, plus an historical survey of the community's politics, were used to identify power and its bases.[4] He found that whereas wealthy, upper-class patricians and social and economic notables had once enjoyed disproportionate power in New Haven, since about 1900 power had shifted mainly into the hands of less-privileged men whose major resources included political connections, office, ethnicity, interest, and energy.

It is noteworthy that Dahl's issue areas tended to emphasize the *public* or *governmental* sector, including nominations for political office, public education, and urban redevelopment. Party nominations, for example, have traditionally been controlled by political professionals, and the ambivalence with which important economic leaders regard local politics is well known. Public education and urban redevelopment are probably somewhat more salient for such leaders, but they are supported by public funds and administered under the aegis of elected or appointed boards and politicians and their administrative aides. There is some question about the saliency of these issues for the most powerful economic leaders.[5] Contrast them with a common problem facing communities today, attracting new industry. Such a decision tends to be essentially private, with the impetus and the funds typically provided by local business elements. Local government may contribute a piece of property or some form of tax concession, but the main inducements come from economic leaders. There are probably no purely private or public issues in community politics, but some criterion such as their ultimate source of funds and legitimacy might enable one to differentiate public from private types. A panel of decisions including both types would seem to provide a more valid basis for generalizations about the over-all structure of community power.

Despite political scientists' intense criticism of the reputational method of identifying power, Dahl's study did not compare the results of this method with those obtained by the decisional method. Here again, further research was suggested by certain inevitable lacunae in existing studies. The incremental thrust of behavioralism is seen once more in the fact that we were able to incorporate in our own work two or three such neglected aspects of power structure research.[6] These included the use of a panel of decisions embracing both public and private issues; a systematic comparison of the results of the reputational and decisional methods; and an attempt to compare political values, pluralism, and power structures in two communities simultaneously. Since time, theory, methodology, and decisions (four of which were the same in both communities) were, so to speak, held constant, it was possible to determine how power structure is affected by such important variables as a community's industrial base, social class, political structure, and its attending "civic psychology."

Guiding criteria for the selection of decisions were three: *significance*, that is, they must have broad scope in terms of effect on the entire community and must involve substantial amounts of money; *representativeness*, that is, they should encompass several substantive fields, roughly typical of the whole spectrum of both public and private decisions or issues faced by the two communities; and finally, *continuity*, the decisions should cover a period of at least a decade to provide some historical perspective about changes in the leadership structure.

Our resources permitted us to study a maximum of five decisions in each community. Local newspapers were analyzed for a ten-year period to identify all significant and representative decisions. Fortunately, the highly salient issues not only stood out dramatically but they did not exceed a half dozen in each community. In this sense, we were able to include a high proportion of their significant decisions. Our desire to generalize was also indulged by the fact that four of the five decisions proved to be substantially similar in both communities. They were: school bond issue, flood control project, new industry, and new hospital facilities. I would judge, moreover, that given recent national population and economic trends, the new school, new industry, and, to a somewhat lesser extent, the new hospital decisions, have been common in most American cities during the past decade.

These decisions had a broad and vital influence on their communities, and all required from $100,000 to $1,300,000 to carry them through. The new industry decisions, we believed, would theoretically engage most of the powerful economic leaders in the community. One of the hospital issues was also defined as private because the necessary funds ($850,000) were raised by a voluntary fund drive. This definition illustrates an inevitable problem of field research: the difficulty of maintaining logically consistent categories. The hospital is part of Edgewood's local government; a committee of its council is formally charged with its supervision. Yet the customary board of distinguished private citizens in truth runs the hospital. The voluntary fund drive; the dominance of hospital affairs by the private board; and the community's private perspective of the hospital provided the rationale for defining the issue as private. Since we wanted to differentiate leaders in terms of the kinds of decisions in which they participated, and more important, to include decisions that would putatively engage both political and economic figures, this was an important point. We also wanted to test the elitist finding that political leaders were controlled by a covert economic elite.

Our findings in Riverview and Edgewood enable us to contribute something to these kinds of questions. We found that selective participation is characteristic of community leaders, particularly when only the " most influential " members of the power structure are compared. Tables 1 and 2 show that whereas public decisions mainly engage political leaders and their appointees, private issues evoke a broader scope of participation, but they are usually dominated by economic leaders.

The type of decision obviously influences participation and attending ascriptions of power. Public decisions are not always salient for economic leaders. In the school decisions, for example, only in Riverview are any economic leaders nominated as highly influential participants. In both communities, specialist types (composed mainly of professional men and their wives) dominate the issue. On the other hand, essentially private issues such as new industries and the hospital issue in Edgewood are usually dominated by economic leaders. In quantitative terms, for example, economic leaders in these issues have a total of forty-one of the most influential attributes, while their political counterparts have a total of only sixteen of them.

TABLE 1   Participation of "most influential" decision-makers, Edgewood *

| | Leaders | | |
Decision	Political (9)	Economic (14)	Specialist (13)
Flood control	Dodd 6		
	Woods 4		
	King 4		
Municipal building	King 5		
	Wells 5		
New hospital	Eberhart 2	Remington 9	Stein 7
		Hughes 3	
New industry	King 3	Hadwen 11	
	Eberhart 2	Prince 10	
		Remington 6	
		Williams 4	
		Dunn 4	
School bond issue			Hanson 5
			Hollis 3

* Only individuals receiving two or more nominations are included in this table. "Most influential" here means that other participants regard them as having exercised the most weight in the decision.

Our research suggests that while economic leaders occasionally participate in public issues, they often do so as ambivalent members of committees formed by the mayor to give a patina of nonpartisanship to the issue. In both communities, the private decisions evoked participation of more than twice as many economic leaders as did most purely governmental decisions—for example, flood control, housing, and municipal building.

Not only do such decisions not attract many economic leaders, but when they do, such leaders tend to play a

TABLE 2   Participation of "most influential" decision-makers, Riverview *

Decision	Leaders		
	Political (10)	Economic (19)	Specialist (6)
Hospital	Wolchak 7	Cavenaugh 7	Baxter 4
	Morrow 7	Armstrong 4	
	O'Brian 3		
Flood control	Morrow 6	Armstrong 2	
	Riley 6		
	O'Brian 2		
Housing authority	O'Brian 5	Armstrong 2	
	Morrow 4		
New industry	Adams 5	Cavenaugh 10	Baxter 3
	O'Brian 4	Mason 4	
		Porter 4	
		Patriarch 4	
		Duncan 4	
		Armstrong 3	
School bond issue		Mason 8	Fischer 7
		Armstrong 3	Baxter 6

* Only individuals receiving two or more nominations are included.

minor role. There is certainly no evidence of covert economic control. Some of the reasons are: the ideological perspectives of economic leaders, which include anti-federal or anti-state spending values; and the belief that local politics is not a very prestigeful activity which brings them into contact with men whose social backgrounds are different from their own. These judgments rest in part on Tables 3 and 4, which compare the values and social statuses of political and economic elites.

TABLE 3 Variations in leaders' political orientations

		Proportion agreeing	
		Political (19)	Economic (33)
1	"That government which governs least governs best."	59	55
2	"We have moved too far away from those fundamental principles that made America great."	41	55
3	"One of the biggest problems with the world is that people don't work hard enough any more."	58	60
4	"Democracy depends fundamentally on the existence of free enterprise."	84	89
5	"On the whole, labor unions are doing a lot of good in this country."	62	48

Noteworthy differences between the two groups appear on the items concerning the alleged abandoning of "fundamental principles" and the role of labor unions.* In

* One explanation for the surprising results regarding the first "anti-government" item is that conservative (sixty-six per cent Republican) Edgewood's political leaders were mainly small businessmen, eighty per cent of whom agreed with this judgment about government's proper role. In Riverview, where political leaders were, with rare exception, Democratic and of somewhat lower social status, the responses to this particular item were: political leaders, forty per cent; economic, fifty-three per cent.

each, political leaders are somewhat more "liberal" than their economic counterparts. When combined with the class differences shown in Table 4, such differences provide some explanation of the tendency for the two groups to participate in different kinds of decisions. We found that when they do combine, as in the new industry and school decisions, they tend to regard each other competitively.

TABLE 4   Social and economic status of Edgewood and Riverview political and economic elites

	Political (19)	Economic (33)
Education: 16 or more years	32%	53%
Time in community: over 20 years	84	87
Fathers' occupation: white collar or higher	78	81
Income: over $10,000	59	84
Membership in organizations: 3 or more	84	84
Political affiliation: Republican	58	80

In this study, class was determined by education and occupational status. By these indexes, economic leaders enjoy somewhat higher class status, which provides some explanation for different patterns of participation among the two groups of leaders. Economic leaders generally viewed local political office and its incumbents with some condescension, and those who did assume political office were likely to be small, marginal businessmen. This conclusion is also supported by economic leaders' nominations to the reputational scale (see Tables 5 and 6), where (with the exception of Riverview's mayor) they tended to de-emphasize the power of elected officials.

In sum, our research suggests that generalizations about community power structure must be based upon a varied and comprehensive panel of decisions which will theoretically evoke participation of what seem to be the most significant groups within the power structure: political, economic and specialist leaders.

Reputational and Decisional Power

An intriguing question and one of our explicit research objectives is the relative validity of the two most common methods of identifying powerful community leaders. Does the reputational method merely isolate those whose social and/or occupational statuses and attending visibility and prestige *should* give them the power to "move things," despite opposition? Or does it identify men who have used their power resources? Is there, in effect, a crucial difference between potential and overt power?

An obvious way to answer such questions is to compare the results obtained by each method. The relationships between them in Edgewood and Riverview are shown in Tables 5 and 6.

The combined overlap rate is about fifty-five per cent. It is important to note, moreover, that I have used a very rigorous test here in which only the most powerful decision-makers (those found to be overtly active in two or more decisions) provide the base against which the reputational findings are set. Lengthening the reputational lists to include, say, another fourteen men and comparing them with *all* decision-makers, that is, all those active in one or more decisions, would undoubtedly have produced a higher ratio of overlapping.

Such evidence permits the conclusion that the reputational instrument will identify more than half of those in the upper reaches of the community power structure. More important, perhaps, it seems to include somewhat different kinds of power-holders, namely those who tend to play a behind-the-scenes role in community affairs—for

TABLE 5 Nominations by decisional and reputational methods, Edgewood

Decision-makers *	(Decs.)	Influentials	(Noms.)	Overlap
Clinton Woods	(4)	Jonathan Davis	(20)	No
Robert King	(4)	Don Remington	(18)	Yes
Frank Moore	(3)	R. G. White	(17)	No
George Parker	(3)	Robert Williams	(17)	Yes
Robert Williams	(3)	John Wainwright	(16)	No
Joseph Wells	(3)	Henry Turner	(15)	No
Don Remington	(2)	R. F. Prince	(14)	Yes
George Albright	(2)	John Dunn	(13)	No
Ben Eberhart	(2)	George Parker	(12)	Yes
Mrs. Thompson	(2)	Robert King	(12)	Yes
R. F. Prince	(2)	Harold Carter	(12)	No
George Reeder	(2)	Anthony Hadwen	(12)	No
John Dodd	(2)	Allen Kimbrough	(12)	No
Robert Evans	(2)	Ben Eberhart	(10)	Yes

* For illustrative convenience, only the "most powerful" of the decision-makers, i. e. those active in two or more decisions, are included here.

example, heads of the largest local corporations. The decisional method, on the other hand, tends to focus mainly on those whom I have called "legmen," that is, leaders who play highly-visible and overt roles in major issues. Such roles are often delegated to them by the heads of the banks and corporations in which they work. The latter's support for a proposed community program was decisive, and was usually secured informally before any public announcement of the decision was made. At this time, the over-all campaign strategy was outlined, committees were designated, and individuals were assigned

TABLE 6   Nominations by decisional and reputational methods, Riverview

Decision-makers *	(Decs.)	Influentials	(Noms.)	Overlap
Ted O'Brian	(5)	Ted O'Brian	(17)	Yes
Fred Morrow	(4)	Richard Cavenaugh	(13)	Yes
Kenneth Armstrong	(4)	Dick Mason	(13)	Yes
Richard Cavenaugh	(3)	Robert Carr	(12)	No
Frank Baxter	(3)	Kenneth Armstrong	(12)	Yes
John Wolchak	(2)	Frank Baxter	(10)	Yes
Walter King	(2)	Fred Schwartz	(9)	No
Dick Mason	(2)	John Riley	(8)	No
Fred Rivers	(2)	Fred Rivers	(7)	Yes
Elmer Riddell	(2)	Ted Johnson	(7)	No
Frank Patriarch	(2)	Fred Morrow	(5)	Yes

* For comparative facility, only those decision-makers who participated in two or more issues are compared with the first eleven (of fourteen) influentials.

various roles. Younger men were given the opportunity to demonstrate their leadership qualifications, in positions that nicely matched their statuses in their own work organizations.

It is important to emphasize that legmen do have power; their active public role in local affairs should not be underestimated. Nevertheless, the vital stage in the decisional process is often the initial " to-do-or-not-to-do " stage, and our research suggests that the reputational method is more likely to identify the kinds of men who have the resources required for this role. As some other studies have found, the most powerful local leaders are often generalists, performing a kind of strategic function which includes defining and organizing major community issues. They tend to be older than their more active colleagues; they enjoy higher social status; they have lived in the community longer; they have higher positions in large corporate organizations; they have substantially higher incomes; and they are more likely to be Republicans. Only regarding educational achievement are they less advantaged than the active decision-makers. While they are not always overtly active, their power is substantial. As one legman put it: "If they aren't behind you, you just aren't going anywhere."

The use of the "overlapping" method is warranted in another way: it helps us determine the degree to which the power structure tends toward the *pluralist* (highly-competitive, issue-specialized) or the *elitist* (monistic, centralized, issue-generalized) end of the continuum. Pluralists have argued that the amount of overlapping among local elites on various substantive issues is a valid test of pluralism-elitism. If leadership is found to be fragmented according to the type of issue involved, the case for pluralism remains valid. On the other hand, if the power of leaders spreads across several types of issues, the system tends toward elitism. As with consensus, no precise cut-off points are specified to indicate at what point the system takes on one or the other of these characterizations. In my own research, the judgment of reasonable men as to the meaning of a "significant" amount of overlap provided an operational criterion. Finding an overlap of thirty per cent among nine communities (see Table 7), ranging in size from 200,000 (Madison) to 6,000 (Edgewood), I concluded that this was a significant degree of overlap and that the tendency toward elitism was inversely associated with size.

Looking specifically at Edgewood and Riverview, our judgment and the amount of overlapping found among

TABLE 7 Decisional overlap among elites in selected cities

Community	Overlap in per cent	Population
New Haven	6	100,000 and over
Madison	19	"
Syracuse	36	"
Racine	29	75,000-100,000
Kenosha	52	50,000- 75,000
Green Bay	11	"
Riverview	32	10,000 and under
Edgewood	39	"
Bennington	39	"

issues and between the two instruments indicate that the structure of power was somewhat more elitist in Riverview. Table 8 adds one bit of supporting evidence.

The data show that participation and reputed influence are significantly associated in Riverview. Almost two-thirds of the active leaders rank high in reputational power. One of the two men who ranked low has recently retired; had the study been carried out a few years earlier, when he was actively involved in the flood control issue, he would probably have been included among the leaders. Generally speaking, however, overt power in Riverview is nicely associated with reputational power.

In Edgewood, the picture is less clear. Nearly half of the decision-makers are ranked high on reputed power, but about thirty per cent of those who were most overtly active are ranked low. These findings probably reflect basic differences in the two power structures. As noted earlier, power in Riverview is more concentrated and hence more visible; there is less difference between overt and reputed power. In Edgewood, power is shared to a

TABLE 8 Involvement in decisions and influential nominations, Edgewood and Riverview, in per cent

| | Reputed influence | | | | | |
| | High | | Medium | | Low | |
Participation *	Edge-wood	River-view	Edge-wood	River-view	Edge-wood	River-view
High	47 (8)	64 (9)	24 (4)	21 (3)	29 (5)	14 (2)
Medium	12 (2)	31 (4)	53 (9)	23 (3)	35 (6)	46 (6)
Low	41 (7)	6 (1)	24 (4)	44 (7)	35 (6)	50 (8)

* After assigning each participant a score for participation and a score for reputed influence, each list was simply divided into thirds with the first third being called High, the second third Medium, and the final third Low. $X^2 - 12.287$, significant at the .05 level.

greater extent; there are more reputational leaders who have highly visible and important organizational statuses, but do not play an active role in local issues. These factors help explain the greater disparity between overt and reputed power found in Edgewood.

Finally, in terms of research economy, it would clearly be unwise not to use the reputational method, which requires only one item and yet identifies more than half of a community's most powerful leaders.[7] Meanwhile by identifying leaders with different bases of power, this method gives us clues about the kinds of roles played by different types of community leaders. It indicates that perceptual differences about community power exist between the more sophisticated activists who are typically asked to make reputational nominations and the community rank-and-file who tend, we found, to impute great power to those who play overt legman roles. Whereas members of the power structure, who generally enjoy highly favorable socio-economic statuses, tend to deprecate politics and the issue-influence of political leaders, rank-and-file members of the community regard them as the most powerful segment of the power structure. This was even true of both new industry decisions, which were clearly dominated by economic leaders. Such differences are based in part upon differences in information and its sources. Rank-and-file members seem to rely more upon press releases and public rituals for the raw material upon which their judgments about power are based, while activists depend upon inside, tough-minded information.

One other means of specifying the relative power of leaders may be presented as an example of behavioral methods. Participation by itself is obviously an incomplete measure of power because it fails to differentiate the amounts of power exercised by leaders in a given decision. Power can be defined more precisely by using weighted levels or intensities of participation. *Initiation, veto*, and *implementation* were therefore defined as indexes of relative power. Initiation is the crucial act of deciding whether community resources will be committed to a given issue. This is probably the most vital stage in the decisional process. Veto is the capacity to prevent or to shift such commitments. And implementation involves the less strategic (but more public) act of carrying out decisions initiated by others. By assigning five points to

TABLE 9 Aggregate power attributes of political and economic decision-makers

Edgewood				Riverview			
Political		Economic		Political		Economic	
King	9	Remington	10	O'Brian	21	Armstrong	12
Woods	8	Williams	9	Morrow	16	Cavenaugh	11
Wells	7	Prince	7	Wolchak	6	Mason	10
Dodd	6	Hadwen	5	Adams	5	Patriarch	6
Moore	3	Dunn	5	Riley	5	Duncan	5
Eberhart	2	Parker	3	Plank	1	Porter	5
Ward	2	Albright	2	Smith	1	Riddell	2
Reeder	2	Thomas	1	Cohen	1	Kruger	2
Parks	1	Miles	1	King	1	Rivers	2
	——	Wilson	1	Thomas	1	King	1
	40	Sherman	1		——	Forrest	1
		Rogers	1		58	Brock	1
		Babcock	1			Morton	1
		Hughes	1			Clark	1
			——			Rowen	1
			48			Wheeler	1
						Muller	1
						Hunter	1
						Waters	1
							——
							65
Average	4.4		3.4		5.8		3.4

initiation, three to veto, and one to implementation, the distribution shown in Table 9 was found.

These data confirm our general conclusions about power in the two communities. Edgewood's economic leaders enjoy an advantage over politicos in total attributes, chiefly because of their large number. In Riverview, although economic leaders again have more attributes than their political rivals, the *averaged* index reveals that the latter are more powerful. More interesting is the intense concentration of power found within all four groups. In every case, the first five leaders have seventy per cent or more of all attributes. Riverview's political figures monopolize fully ninety per cent of the total in their group. Since concentrated power is always more decisive than aggregate power, the conclusion is that Riverview's top political leaders are the most powerful men in either community.

Pluralism and Elitism

The utility of a behavioral approach for analyzing questions of both theoretical and normative significance is suggested by current research regarding pluralism and elitism. The controversy between social scientists concerning the true structure of community power was mentioned earlier. One group maintains that such structures are essentially pluralistic, meaning that power is fragmentized among leaders in terms of the substantive issues with which they are concerned. Competition and bargaining go on among these specialized elites. It is held that the major power resources in community political life are those of political office, interest, ethnicity, and group membership, and that power is based less upon wealth and middle- and upper-class status, than upon political skills, knowledge, and access to the processes by which decisions are made. Pluralists assume that citizens exercise a great deal of indirect influence upon specific issues through their votes for candidates, as well as for specific referenda when these are required. Considerable emphasis is placed upon the weight that political leaders give citizen expectations when decisions are made. Generally, while pluralists recognize that only about one-quarter of citizens play an active political role (usually defined as voting, discussing issues with friends and political officials, attending political meetings, and so on), they tend to conclude that power is broadly shared among leaders and between them and rank-and-file members of the community.

Opposed to this rationale is the elitist hypothesis which maintains that power in the community political arena tends to be concentrated in a small group of leaders (usually economic) who possess unusual amounts of resources, including middle- and upper-class status, greater amounts of education, income, access, organizational memberships, and prestige inherent in their high positions in organizations. Their power is based upon resources that often have greater continuity than those of political leaders, including wealth or control of wealth and high corporate positions. Whereas pluralists maintain that power is issue-specialized, elitists maintain that the power of any elite cuts across several substantive areas. Power in a word is seen to be generalized in scope. Finally, elitists believe that power is essentially a social and collective phenomenon, maintained and exercized through alliances with other individuals of similar interest, ideology, and status. Following organizational theory in which the generalization is that power usually centers in a few hands, elitists assume a similar condition in larger collectivities such as the community.

This outline of the two opposing theories indicates that pluralism closely fits the major assumptions of traditional democratic political philosophy. Even though pluralists emphasize that the representation of mass interests by elected officials is the most that can be expected in an imperfect political world, they also retain the latent expectation that some citizens are politically interested, active, and influential. This follows from their assumption that power is atomized in American politics. Elitism, on the other hand, suggests a different kind of political order, in which inert, politically alienated masses are ruled by elites who manipulate them through propaganda, ceremonials and other mock participation. Elitists emphasize the lack of commitment to voluntary groups that might serve as a barrier between an all-powerful state and the unorganized individuals found in mass society.

The local community seems a good place to test these opposing theories. The extent of citizen participation can be viewed as a valid indicator of pluralism, particularly when augmented by two other pluralist conditions, namely, membership in organizations and organizational participation in the major issues. Contemporary pluralists, of course, recognize that *direct* citizen participation in major issues is limited, yet implicit in both their own assumptions and those of historical pluralism is the expectation that citizens can and will occasionally play an active personal role in local government.

Since its inception in the Middle Ages, pluralism has always had an individualistic cast, aimed at insuring personal liberty against an omnipotent state.[8] The contemporary transfer of its focus to group participation and, particularly, the view that such associations insure individual interests is a recent development reflecting American conditions in which voluntary group membership has been more widespread than in Europe. It must be said, however, that group membership has been overstated in the United States, as revealed by studies using nationwide samples.[9] The current rationale that pluralism triumphs if competition exists among the specialized elites often found in local power structures is also a somewhat new departure. In effect, the theoretical assumptions underlying my own study include the pluralist view that group membership and group activity on behalf of individual members provide valid tests, but that some measure of direct individual participation is also required to honor pluralist themes. The view that competition among the elites within the power structure validates the pluralist hypothesis is rejected, partly because conclusions that seem to make a virtue out of necessity are always suspect.

By using empirical indicators of participation in several decisions, it seemed possible to compare the political cultures of the communities and to place each at some point along a pluralist continuum. This required one initial decision which illustrates problems of categorization in behavioral research. For some time, it seemed that a systematic analysis of participation should make it possible to define the communities precisely as being either pluralist or elitist. I played with the idea of some exact quantitative standard, such as that whenever rank-and-file participation (as measured by voting, attending meetings, discussing the issues with others, and so on) fell below fifty per cent, the community could be designated as having an elitist power structure. While such a standard would be arbitrary, it would follow the quantitative thrust of our research on participation. I was also motivated in part by some exasperation with the failure of social scientists to define more precisely such central concepts as consensus, which V. O. Key has very properly called a magic word. It seemed to me that pluralism similarly needed specification.

It soon became apparent, however, that both logic and the nature of survey data made it advisable to settle for a "more-or-less" approach, in which the communities would be compared with each other using the continuum idea. When one compares two universes, he must be content with scaling them in a more-or-less context. Comparisons with some absolute criterion push both logic and survey analysis beyond their capacity.

Another illustrative methodological problem arises here. Five criteria were used to measure rank-and-file participation: voting, contributing time or money to an issue, discussing it with a friend, attending a meeting, and being a member of a committee dealing with an issue. Initially, since these criteria obviously entail different intensities of participation, I tried to weight them. Here again, difficulties arose. For example, even though serving on a committee should obviously rank high in such a scale, this media was available to only a very limited number of citizens. Discussion with colleagues and a look at indexes commonly used to measure participation resulted in a decision not to attempt to weight the various criteria, even though such precision seemed desirable.

This brief introduction may provide an adequate framework for presenting our findings on pluralism. Figure 1 compares rates of individual participation in the major decisions in both communities.

These data reveal several differences between the communities, as well as some interesting continuities in levels of individual participation for given types of decisions. Average rates are ten per cent in Riverview compared with thirty per cent in Edgewood. Since the national aver-

FIGURE 1

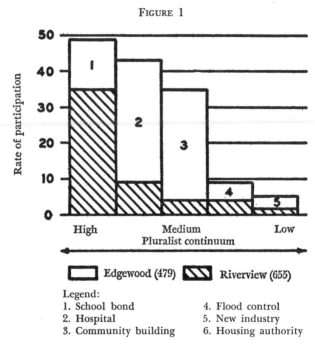

Rate of participation

High   Medium   Low
Pluralist continuum

Edgewood (479)   Riverview (655)

Legend:
1. School bond   4. Flood control
2. Hospital   5. New industry
3. Community building   6. Housing authority

age for such participation is twenty-five per cent, Edgewood fares comparatively well, while Riverview is quite low. The generalization is that Edgewood ranks somewhat more toward the high end of the pluralist continuum, compared with Riverview. However, as expected, neither of these rates proved to be very inspiring. Whether even Edgewood's higher rate of participation qualifies it as a pluralistic political system must be left to individual judgments.

The data show too that certain kinds of decisions, that is, school bond issues and hospital building programs, tend to evoke the most participation among citizens. Rather more political decisions involving subsidies from state and federal agencies, for example, flood control and housing projects, tend to fall at the low end of the scale.

TABLE 10   Comparative voluntary group membership in Edgewood and Riverview

Type of organization	Proportion belonging *	
	Edgewood	Riverview
Social	42 (253)	43 (355)
Service	39 † (258)	30 (246)
Patriotic	22 (108)	21 (144)
Labor	15 † (56)	26 (181)
Professional	11 (25)	8 (62)
Political	7 (32)	7 (46)
Business	5 (22)	3 (30)

* This figure is the proportion of members in the total community sample.

† Significant at .01 level.

Turning to our second indicator of pluralism, organizational membership, Table 10 shows membership patterns to be similar, with two important differences, one of which has suggestive implications for community viability. Service organizations such as civic clubs, heart societies, and the like, have a significantly higher membership rate in Edgewood. Since these types of organizations are the main ones concerned with community improvement and have the largest proportions of highly educated members, the difference seems important. There is also a significant membership difference between the communities in labor organizations. When the comparative *intensities* of membership are compared, we find that Edgewood has a small advantage, thirty-six per cent of the community belonging to three or more organizations compared with thirty-three per cent in Riverview.

Membership, as might be expected, is associated with class status. In both communities a linear relationship was found, in which about two-thirds of upper-class citizens belonging to three or more organizations compared with only one-fifth of those in the lower class. In both communities, two-thirds of lower-class citizens belonged to no organizations, not including church memberships.

These membership rates are close to but somewhat above the national averages found by other researchers. But a more crucial question is whether, in line with pluralist theory, the organizations provide their members a means of access to the decision making process. We, therefore, attempted to determine how actively major local organizations were involved in the ten decisions. Active involvement was defined according to three criteria: passing a resolution for or against the proposed issue; forming a special committee to study the issue; or donating time, money, or some other type of active support to a given decision. Table 11 shows the extent of all types of participation.

Here we find almost twice as high a proportion of organizations active in Edgewood as in Riverview. Perhaps a more significant fact is that ninety per cent of all active organizations participated in only *one* of the five major issues in their respective communities. This suggests that voluntary organizations do not necessarily provide the assumed measure of access. Here, in effect, a basic pluralist assumption is challenged: that even though an individual's direct participation in political decisions is neces-

TABLE 11   Participation of voluntary organizations in ten community decisions

Edgewood (23)		Riverview (29)	
Decision	Number of participations *	Decision	Number of participations
New hospital	10	New hospital	6
School bond issue	2	School bond issue	3
New industry	1	New industry	3
Flood control	1	Flood control	1
Community building	1	Housing Authority	0
Number of organizations participating †	12	Number of organizations participating †	8
Per cent of all organizations	52 **	Per cent of all organizations	28

* Because several organizations participated in more than one decision, the total number of organizations participating is less than the total number of participations.

† "Participation" is determined by three criteria: the organization passed a resolution for or against the decision; it formed a special committee to study or work on the issue; or it donated money, time, or some other type of support.

** Significant at .10 level.

sarily limited, he is saved from impotence because he belongs to organizations which make his will felt by influencing the issues that effect him. No doubt this process often occurs, but it did not occur very frequently in Edgewood and Riverview.

Once again, certain types of decisions inspired the most participation. The hospital building programs were first by a great margin, followed as a poor second by the school bond issue, and in Riverview by the new industry decision. In all, however, voluntary organizations were not very active. The main explanations seem to be that they have rather limited and specific goals, and that their leaders possess considerably less of the hard resources enjoyed by members of the power structure. They did have considerable political sophistication, as evidenced by their accurate nominations to the reputational list. Personally, they knew those in the community who had power, but their organizations played little real part in the major issues.

In summary, the three measures of pluralism in the two communities revealed that direct individual participation in the ten issues was (with the exception of voting) very low; that membership in voluntary associations was similar to that found throughout the nation, with rather less membership than often assumed and with big differences among class strata; and finally, that participation by such organizations was, in effect, only one-fifth of what it might have been, that is, with only three exceptions, the twenty active organizations participated in only one decision each.

It is clear from these findings that the two communities occupy different positions along the pluralist continuum. Here again, several concepts seem useful in determining why this is so. Perhaps one of the most suggestive involves alienation, which may be defined as a condition in which an individual feels personally estranged or disengaged from conventional social values. Widely-shared norms such as equality of opportunity, social mobility, and personal political efficacy may be rejected. Highly alienated individuals may feel themselves outsiders, unable to honor dominant patterns of behavior in a given community. Withdrawal from political affairs has been found to be a common reaction among such groups. There is also some evidence that when they are politically active, they often

TABLE 12 Social class and alienation, in per cent *

| | Class status | | | | | |
| | Upper | | Middle | | Lower | |
	(83) Edgewood	(74) Riverview	(324) Edgewood	(421) Riverview	(80) Edgewood	(169) Riverview
1 Low	34	26	18	14	9	8
2	51	54	32	34	27	28
3 Medium	8	14	22	26	20	15
4	2	3 †	17	17	20	25
5 High	2 †	4	10	6	23	15

* This scale is composed of the following items: 1) " Most decisions in Riverview-Edgewood are made by a small group that pretty much runs the community"; 2) "Anyone in Edgewood-Riverview who wants to gets a chance to have his say about important issues "; 3) " The average man doesn't really have much chance to get ahead today"; 4) " The old saying, ' You can't fight city hall ' is still basically true."

† Significant at .01 level.

play an " anti " role, combining forces to defeat proposals for new schools and fluoridation.[10]

Given their discrete positions regarding pluralism, we would expect to find a larger proportion of highly alienated citizens in Riverview than in Edgewood. But Table 12 shows no significant differences in alienation, and it is clear that we must mainly look elsewhere for an explanation of the different levels of pluralism found in the two communities. The expected linear association between class and alienation offers one rather weak bit of evidence. Very high rates of alienation are found among lower-class citizens in both communities. We also know that Riverview has a significantly higher proportion (twenty-six versus sixteen per cent) of respondents in this category. From this, we can say that the sum total of highly alienated citizens in the community is considerably larger than in Edgewood. This aspect of her political culture partly explains her generally lower level of participation.

Turning to other, and, hopefully, more fruitful evidence, we next consider three variables that seem to be related to participation. These concern the relative amounts of political interest, knowledge, and involvement characterizing the two communities.* Political interest and knowledge are commonly found to be associated with participation; the degree of personal identification or involvement with the community is assumed to be a valid indicator of the disposition to participate. In effect, individuals who feel emotionally attached to their community are more likely to become active in its major decisions. Table 13 indicates that the communities exhibit some differences in this regard.

It is immediately apparent that, compared with leaders, rank-and-file members of both communities have many

---

* "Interest" was determined by scaled responses to a single question on political interest. "Knowledge" was determined by responses to several questions concerning such items as the name of U.S. Senators from New York, local representatives to Albany, and so on. "Involvement" was measured by the question: "While it may not be perfect, this community offers just about everything a person could want."

fewer of these kinds of political resources. Yet, only involvement shows a significant inter-community difference. Over eighty per cent of Edgewood's leaders are closely identified with the community, compared with only fifty-six per cent in Riverview. Comparative rates for followers are seventy-one and forty-seven per cent. *Less than half of Riverview's citizens think the community is a good place in which to live; and the assumption is that this attitude*

TABLE 13   Comparative levels of political interest, knowledge, and community involvement between leaders and rank-and-file

	Edgewood			Riverview		
	Interest	Knowl-edge	Involve-ment	Interest	Knowl-edge	Involve-ment
Leaders (81)	88	98	83	88	99	56
Rank and file (1198)	58	79	71	54	81	47

is one explanation of the lower rates of participation found there.

These data suggest that the two communities have a different civic psychology. Proof of this difference is provided in Table 14, which should be evaluated with the fact in mind that the major correlate of political participation is social class.

That rates of participation differ considerably, and in some cases significantly, within class categories indicates that the communities do indeed have different political cultures. Edgewood generally provides more social support for political action. The differences, moreover, are greatest among the largest middle-class stratum, from which the largest potential number of activists might be expected to come. The mean rates of community participation among all classes are fifty-seven per cent for Edgewood, and only forty-one per cent for Riverview.

TABLE 14   Class and participation, in per cent

Proportion active in one or more decisions					
Upper class		Middle class		Lower class	
Edge-wood	River-view	Edge-wood	River-view	Edge-wood	River-view
(83)	(74)	(324)	(421)	(80)	(169)
57 †	50 †	67 *	42	43	32

* Significant at .01 level.   † Significant at .05 level.

Some Implications of Power Structure Research for Public Administration

The power structure methods reported here are probably adaptable to the analysis of public organizations. It seems entirely practicable, for example, to use the reputational and decisional methods to determine the structure of power and influence within an organization. Given the tendency of decision making to be channeled along the lines of functional specialization, it would be necessary to select one's decisions with great care. Otherwise, one's labors might only reveal the banal truth that financial experts monopolize issues dealing with money, while military men dominate those involving violence. Yet, in any organization there are some highly generalized kinds of decisions which become competitive across functional boundaries. In the university, for example, assuming some faculty participation, such decisions might include whether to double the size of the student body, to initiate a space research program, or to establish a new branch college in a nearby metropolitan area. Such decisions might provide a valid basis for judgments about the relative power of individuals and of the various skill groups within the organization.

We also saw earlier that power structure research has been used to analyze the role of public administrators in community decision making. In addition, as the next chapter shows, power structure analysis can be combined with support theory to compare and explain the effectiveness of various kinds of community organizations.

3
Behavioral Research
in Organizational Effectiveness

We can now turn more directly to behavioral research in an organizational context. This research, which is part of the same power structure study, concerns a theory and a method of dealing with the question of organizational effectiveness. What kinds of variables are critical for the capacity of an organization to accomplish its manifest functions? I am going to be oversimple here and assume that the main objective of organizations is to carry out their official mission. Even though some of us believe that survival, growth, and individual career aspirations provide at least equally compelling motives, in the interests of research strategy we will disregard such latent objectives.

One theoretical frame for analyzing effectiveness is so-called "support theory" which holds that all organizations depend upon their environment for certain needed resources (including a market for their product), and that the capability of any organization is importantly a function of the extent to which it is able to capture such resources.[1] (This is a tautological proposition, but such is true of many research hypotheses and impairs neither their value nor their validity as analytical tools.) The support hypothesis is similar to John M. Gaus' ecological conception of administration set down in this series in 1947.[2] It posits a functional interdependence between any given organization and its environment. Like the theory which sees personal interaction as a system of exchange for approval and consensual validation, support theory concerns itself with bargaining between the organization and relevant external groups. From these groups the organization draws the resources of skill, money, and prestige necessary for its survival and growth. In return, it provides the community with some socially valued service or product.

Support theory is a useful analytical construct because it asks revealing questions about an organization. The answers tell us much that we could not learn from a microscopic research perspective. The class composition of the major clientele group or the governing body of a voluntary association or a work organization will, for example, often strongly affect its operating rationale. This is nicely apparent in the difference between private and publicly supported hospitals in the United States. Middle-class people often have a horror of being placed in public hospitals, which may be regarded as déclassé, last-resort places for indigents. Private hospitals, on the other hand, have usually been able to attract more prestigeful clients, and their boards usually include some of the most powerful men and women in the community. Partly for these reasons, private hospitals are often relatively more successful in attracting superior professional workers. Their prestige in the larger community has an immediate impact on their operational effectiveness. Community support, in effect, has legitimated the hospital's role, and given it the patina of superiority that privately-fostered institutions often enjoy in our society.

Support theory also has the advantage of generality: it can be applied to many organizations regardless of their mission and their locus in the socio-governmental structure. The interdependence of federal agencies and their clientele groups is well known. An explanation, for example, of the annual appropriation difficulties of internationally oriented organizations such as the Agency for International Development (AID) or the United States Information Service (USIS) lies in part in their lack of a strong base of interest group support in the United States. Our attempts to learn precisely why this is so tell us a great deal about the conditions of organizational viability in American society.

Some such theoretical guidelines were used to guide research on two hospitals in Edgewood and Riverview.[3] The objective was to determine whether there was a relationship between the effectiveness of the hospitals and the extent to which each was tied into the local power structure through social interactions and joint organizational memberships existing between their board members and powerful leaders in the community. Earlier research had revealed that one hospital was more effective than the other. Next, it was necessary to establish empirically that a differential level of support did in fact characterize the two organizations. The accompanying tables indicate that this was indeed so. We began by asking whether the hospitals in Edgewood and Riverview differ regarding the amount and kind of monetary support they receive. The data in Table 15 show that there are substantial differences between them, one hospital clearly receiving less from its community than the other. On a dollars-per-bed

TABLE 15   Funds received by the two hospitals from all external community sources, 1949-1960

Source of funds	Edgewood Memorial (75 beds in 1960)		Riverview District (51 beds in 1960)	
	Amounts received	Per cent of total	Amounts received	Per cent of total
Governmental appro-priations	$ 215,000	18	$305,349	72
Bond issues and notes	0	..	79,000	19
Voluntary fund drives	724,231	60	0	..
Contributions and in-crease in endowments	265,378	22	38,144	9
	$1,204,609	100.0	$422,493	100.0

basis, Edgewood Memorial received almost twice as much ($16,063) as Riverview District ($8,304). The disparity becomes even greater when total funds are calculated on a per capita basis. The Riverview hospital received only $28 while its counterpart received $145. On these bases Edgewood has been much more generous in the money contributed to its hospital.

The data also reveal that over eighty per cent of the funds received by Edgewood Memorial have come from private, voluntary donations. Even though the hospital is legally owned by the community and operated by a board of managers appointed by the mayor, the money provided for its support has come mainly from voluntary fund drives and private donations, that is, from nongovernmental channels. This does not mean, of course, that the hospital has never considered supporting itself through public financing or that this alternative is for some reason ruled out. At one point, before the construction of the new building, the village board had agreed to raise additional funds through a bond issue. A supplementary fund drive made this unnecessary. It is quite possible that future construction may be paid for in this fashion, but the dominant pattern of monetary support has been one of voluntary contributions and bequests.

It might seem that the explanations for such differential patterns of support are obvious. Edgewood has been able to provide generously for its hospital without major reliance upon the tax powers of local government simply because it is wealthy. Riverview is a poorer community, and lacking any great wealth, has had to turn to public financing to support its hospital. Expenditures have come from taxes collected from local property owners and industries. While this is certainly a partial explanation, it clearly does not account for the entire difference.

If differences in what is available in Edgewood and Riverview were sufficient to explain why one hospital has received less in the way of financial support than the other, we would expect total community support for the hospital in Riverview to be at least equal to or greater than that in Edgewood. The hospital competes with other local organizations and businesses for a share of the citizen's dollar, and it could be that Riverview District has, in fact, received a share comparable to Edgewood Memorial. However, as Table 16 shows, this has not been the case.

The total volume of retail sales in the two communities during the decade 1949 to 1960, which gives us one measure of family expenditures for nonhospital goods and services, is shown in the table. By dividing this figure into the total monetary support received by the two hospitals, we can compare the relative financial effort of each community. As can be seen, Riverview has an index number of .31 while Edgewood's is .71. In sum, when expenditures on the hospital are expressed as a proportion of ex-

TABLE 16 Community monetary support index: total monetary support of the hospital as a proportion of total volume of retail sales, 1949-1960

	Total retail sales * (Col. 1)	Total monetary support of hospitals † (Col. 2)	(Col. 2 ÷ Col. 1)
Edgewood	$170,669,000	$1,204,609	.71
Riverview	137,429,000	422,493	.31

* *Sales Management*, " Survey of Buying Power," 1949–60.
† *Ibid.*, Table 1, p. 9.

penditures on other goods and services in the community, Edgewood has made over twice the financial effort to support its hospital that Riverview has made.

Another approach to this problem is to ask: What about those people in Riverview who do have money? Have they been as willing to contribute to the hospital as their counterparts in Edgewood? Using reported family income in 1960, number of individuals in the family age twenty and over in 1961, and home ownership to construct a scale of economic well-being, respondents were compared in terms of voluntary donations to the hospitals. The results are summarized in Table 17.

At every economic level, respondents in Riverview were less likely to report a donation to the hospital than those in Edgewood. Furthermore, the difference between these groups, significant at the .01 level, is greatest for those at the highest end of the economic well-being scale. Compared with their counterparts in Edgewood, those

TABLE 17 Relationship between economic well-being and voluntary contributions to the hospitals in Edgewood and Riverview, in per cent

	Voluntary contributions			
Economic well-being	Edgewood		Riverview	
Lowest	28	(40)	9	(23)
Low	43	(81)	40	(101)
Medium-low	41 †	(87)	28	(170)
Medium-high	45 *	(143)	31	(204)
High	74	(69)	61	(79)
Highest	91 *	(45)	43	(23)

* Significant at .01.   † Significant at .05.

with the most to give in Riverview have been least likely to do so. The table also makes clear, however, that in each community some individuals in every economic range have contributed voluntarily to their hospital.

What about community support of the hospitals through volunteer services? Auxiliaries and other volunteer organizations perform a number of important hospital services. In addition to contributing money and equipment, these groups frequently perform such duties as wrapping bandages, serving meals, cleaning up the hospital's grounds, and the like, services which leave the regular staff free to concentrate on more vital work.

As shown in Table 18, the amounts of volunteer work received by each hospital differ greatly. Comparatively few people in Riverview when asked, " Have you ever worked in the (community) hospital in any capacity? " spontaneously reported that they had done volunteer work of some kind. In Edgewood thirteen per cent of those interviewed mentioned that they had contributed volunteer service to their hospital. The small number of cases, particularly in Riverview, makes any detailed analysis of these responses impossible, but these figures reinforce

TABLE 18   Per cent of those interviewed who spontaneously mentioned that they had done volunteer work in the hospital

Edgewood (494)	Riverview (704)
13 *	2

* Significant at .01.

earlier qualitative observations. People and organizations in Riverview have been much less likely to give their time and money to the community hospital than those in Edgewood.

An equally important question is whether all groups in both communities have shown an equal willingness to become patients in their respective hospitals. When people need care, do they usually go to the local hospital or do they go elsewhere? Other hospitals are available within thirty minutes' driving time from both communities. Given this fact, plus the economic opportunity to be able to make such a choice, how do the hospitals compare in this respect?

The data indicate that those who can afford it have been

much more likely to go outside the community for hospitalization in Riverview than have those with similar incomes in Edgewood. Looking at those who are native to each community, and thus most likely to have faced a choice between the local and a nonlocal hospital, we find in Table 19 little difference between the two communities at the bottom ends of the economic scale. As might

TABLE 19   Hospitalization experience of community natives controlled for economic security, in per cent

| Economic well-being | Local hospital experience | | | |
	Edgewood		Riverview	
Low	90	(17)	82	(30)
Medium-low	92	(22)	94	(67)
Medium-high	90 *	(18)	79	(69)
High	90 †	(18)	59	(19)

* Significant at .05.   † Significant at .10.

be expected, a very high proportion of those in the low or medium-low categories who have had any hospitalization experience have had it locally. Moreover, at the high end of the scale in Edgewood, the proportion of natives who have been patients in the community hospital remains at the same level. But this does not hold for Riverview; only about sixty per cent of high-income respondents picked Riverview District, compared with ninety per cent of their counterparts in Edgewood.

Bases of Differential Support

Having seen that the hospitals have in fact received different levels of support, we can now turn to an explanation of this condition. The theoretical assumption, it will be recalled, is that the explanation lies in differences in the extent to which the governing boards of the two hospitals are tied into the local power structure through joint membership in organizations and social ties.

Differences between boards appear when we look at the memberships shared by their members with other influentials in the communities. With one exception, as Table 20 shows, every hospital board member in Edgewood is a director or chief official in an organization with one or more other community leaders. Three members, R. G. White, Scott Maxwell, and Frank Thomas, have held more key positions in other organizations (four each) than any other member. The overlapping directorships of the three women members of the board have been limited to one organization, the Country Club, while one member, Tom Mason, has not held a key position in any other organization in the community. The average number of key positions held by Edgewood board members is 2.00, slightly less than the average score of the community leaders (2.43).

Both banks in Edgewood are directly represented on the hospital board as is Greater Edgewood Industries (GEI), a key organization in the community. The United Fund provides another point of overlap as do the Chamber of Commerce and the Rotary Club. In short, there are a number of instances where one or more members of the hospital board hold key positions in organizations with one or more community leaders.

Another striking feature of Table 20 is the extent to which decision-makers, both those on the board like White, Remington, and Maxwell, and nonhospital board

TABLE 20 Overlapping directorships of Edgewood Memorial Board "most nominated" influentials and decision-makers who participated in three or more decisions

Names	Occupations	Social class	Citizens Bank	First Trust Co.	Greater Edgewood Industries	United Fund	Chamber of Commerce	Country Club	Rotary Club	Mental Health Association	County Democratic Committee	Episcopal Church	First Congregational Church	Total Score
Hospital Board:														
R. G. White*	Banker	II	x	:	x	x	x	:	:	:	:	:	:	4
Frank Thomas	Business Executive	I	:	:	:	x	:	:	x	x	:	:	x	4
Tom Hughes	Businessman	II	:	x	:	:	:	:	:	:	:	x	:	2
Mrs. Reed	(hus.) Engineer	I	:	:	:	:	:	x	:	:	:	:	:	1
George Wilson	Businessman	II	x	:	:	:	x	:	x	:	:	:	:	3
Tom Mason	Engineer	I	:	:	:	:	:	:	:	:	:	:	:	0
William Rogers	Engineer	I	:	:	:	:	:	:	:	:	x	:	:	1
Mrs. Pamela Thomas	(hus.) Stock Broker	II	:	:	:	:	:	x	:	:	:	:	:	1
Mrs. G. Parker	(hus.) Lawyer*	I	:	:	:	:	:	x	:	:	:	:	:	1
Don Remington*	Business Executive	II	:	:	x	:	:	:	:	:	:	:	:	1
(Scott Maxwell)[1]	Banker	I	x	:	x	x	:	:	x	:	:	:	:	4
Sub Total			3	1	3	3	2	3	3	1	1	1	1	22

TABLE 20—Continued

Names	Occupations	Social class	Citizens Bank	First Trust Co.	Greater Edgewood Industries	United Fund	Chamber of Commerce	Country Club	Rotary Club	Mental Health Association	County Democratic Committee	Episcopal Church	First Congregational Church	Total Score
Influentials:*														
Jonathan Davis	Business Executive	II		x	x	x		x						4
Harold Carter	Bank Clerk-Mayor	III			x									1
Robert King†	Small Businessman-Ex-Mayor	II			x		x		x		x			4
Allen Kimbrough	Business Executive	II			x									1
Henry Turner	Business Executive	II		x		x	x							3
Bob Williams	Business Executive	I		x										1
John Dunn	Banker	I		x	x									2
Ben Eberhart	Businessman-Town Supervisor	III		x	x						x			3
Anthony Hadwen	Banker	II		x	x	x								3
G. Parker	Lawyer	I	x		x			x	x					4
R. F. Prince	Newspaper Editor	II			x	x			x			x		4
John Wainwright	Business Executive	I	x										x	2
Sub Total			2	6	9	4	2	2	3	0	2	1	1	32

The org columns (Citizens Bank through First Congregational Church) fall under the heading *Organizations*.

TABLE 20—Continued

Names	Occupations	Social class	Citizens Bank	First Trust Co.	Greater Edgewood Industries	United Fund	Chamber of Commerce	Country Club	Rotary Club	Mental Health Association	Country Democratic Committee	Episcopal Church	First Congregational Church	Total Score
Decision Makers: †														
Clinton Woods	City Attorney-Politician	I	...	...	...	...	...	...	...	x	x	...	...	2
Joseph Wells	Businessman-Accountant	I	...	...	...	...	...	...	...	...	x	...	...	0
Sub Total			0	0	0	0	0	0	0	1	1	0	0	2
Totals ²			5	7	12	7	4	5	6	2	4	2	2	56

* "Most nominated" influentials.
† Decision-makers who participated in 3 or more of the 5 decisions.
¹ Maxwell was on the Hospital Board for 17 years until he left the community in February 1961.
² For each directorship or office held by a board member or leader, a score of 1 was assigned. These were then totaled. These scores include only organizations in which there is an overlap between board members and leaders.

members, are integrated in terms of their directorships. All but three of the " most-nominated " leaders (N = 14) belong to GEI, and six of them are also directors of the First Trust Company. Two of the most-nominated influentials, Allen Kimbrough and Bob Williams, are not officials in GEI, but they are on the board of First Trust and their sons are directors of GEI. Moreover, of the four leaders who may be classified as politicians and local government officials, that is, Harold Carter, Robert King, Ben Eberhart, and Clinton Woods, three are directors of GEI.

When we look at Riverview board members in terms of their membership in key positions, a somewhat different picture emerges, as Table 21 shows. Only one member of this board, Richard Cavenaugh, holds a key position in the economic institutions of the community. Not only is he on the board of directors of the largest bank in Riverview and of the small savings and loan association, but he is also a director of the largest manufacturing company. He holds more key positions (five) than any other individual on either board. The other bank in Riverview is not directly represented and two of the board members, Mrs. Frank King and Alex Schmidt, share no directorships in common with the community leaders shown here. A third, Reverend Frank Baxter, shares only his position in the United Fund. The average score of the members of the hospital board in Riverview is 1.86 and compares with an average score of 1.78 for the leaders shown in the table.

When we look only at community leaders, the degree of integration through overlapping directorships found in Edgewood is missing. The greatest area of overlap is the Chamber of Commerce and the United Fund, but several of the most-nominated influentials, including Fred Rivers,

TABLE 21 Overlapping directorships of Riverview District Board "most nominated" influentials and decision-makers who participated in three or more decisions

Name	Occupation	Social class	Riverview Trust Co.	Riverview Savings & Loan Assn.	United Fund	Chamber of Commerce	Episcopal Church	County Democratic Committee	City Council	Red Cross	School Board	Peterson Furniture	Total Scores
					Organizations								
Hospital Board:													
Frank Baxter *†	Minister	I			x								1
Richard Cavenaugh *†	Banker	I	x	x		x	x					x	5
Mrs. F. King	(hus.) Business Executive	II								x			1
Harold Plank	Personnel Mgr.– Politician	II							x	x	x		3
John Wolchak	Chief Clerk (R.R.)	III			x			x					2
Fred Rivers *†	Businessman	II						x					1
Alex Schmidt	Physiotherapist	II											0
Sub Total			1	1	2	1	1	2	1	2	1	1	13

* "Most nominated" influentials.   † Decision-makers who participated in 3 or more of 5 issues studied.

1 For each directorship or office held by a board member or leader, a score of 1 was assigned. These were then totaled. These scores include only organizations in which there is an overlap between board members and leaders.

Table 21—Continued

| | | Social class | Organizations | | | | | | | | | | | |
Name	Occupation		Riverview Trust Co.	Riverview Savings & Loan Assn.	United Fund	Chamber of Commerce	Episcopal Church	County Democratic Committee	City Council	Red Cross	School Board	Peterson Furniture	Total Scores
Influentials: *													
Fred Schwartz	Small Businessman	II	...	...	...	...	...	...	...	...	...	...	0
John Riley	Small Businessman	III	x	...	...	...	...	...	...	...	...	...	1
Ted O'Brian†	Mayor-Stock Clerk	IV	...	...	...	...	...	x	x	...	...	...	2
Ted Johnson	Business Executive	II	x	...	x	x	...	...	...	...	...	x	4
Kenneth Armstrong†	Newspaper Editor	I	...	x	x	x	x	...	...	...	...	...	4
Robert Carr	Businessman	II	...	...	...	x	...	...	...	...	...	...	1
Dick Mason	Banker	II	...	...	x	...	...	...	...	...	x	...	2
Fred Morrow†	Lawyer	I	...	...	...	...	...	...	...	...	...	...	0
George McGuire	Supermarket Mgr.	III	...	...	...	x	...	...	...	...	...	...	1
Kenneth Swanson	Business Executive	II	...	...	...	x	...	...	...	...	...	...	1
Frank O'Connor	Lawyer	I	...	...	x	...	...	x	...	...	...	...	2
Sub Total			2	1	4	5	1	2	1	0	1	1	18
Totals [1]			3	2	6	6	2	4	2	2	2	2	31

John Riley, and Ted O'Brian, are directors or officials of neither. The two men most active in the major decisions, Ted O'Brian and Fred Morrow, were not associated with any of the other leaders as directors of these organizations. In short, leaders as well as board members in Edgewood have more of an opportunity to influence each other through mutual organizational memberships than they have in Riverview.

Striking evidence that these connections reflect a deeper and closer social network is presented in Table 22. Almost everyone in Edgewood who was active in one or more of the five decisions and/or was nominated as an influential, reported knowing one or more of the hospital board members socially. That is, an overwhelming majority of the community leaders in Edgewood exchange home visits with various members of the board. The data also reveal that these social contacts are not limited to only two or three members of the board. *All* board members have close social ties with some of these leaders and there is considerable overlap among these ties. Almost sixty per cent of the leaders reported knowing three or more board members socially. The two members who are best known socially by community leaders are Don Remington, one of the most-nominated influentials, and Mrs. George Parker, whose husband was another of the most-nominated leaders.

The data show again the relatively greater homogeneity and integration of the board and the community leadership network in Edgewood. Almost all of the decision-makers, over eighty per cent, are in either social class I or class II, and all of the board members are in one of these two classes. Many of the community leaders socialize with hospital board members, and, by implication, with

TABLE 22   Social connections (exchange of home visits) between community leaders and hospital board members in Edgewood

		Hospital board members									
Community leaders †	Social class	Mrs. Reed	Wilson	Mason	Rogers	Mrs. Thomas	Hughes	Mrs. Parker	White	Thomas	Remington
1	II	..	self	..	..	..	..	..	x	..	..
2	I	x	..	..	..	x	..	x	x	..	x
3	I	..	..	..	..	x	..	..	..	..	..
4 *	II	..	..	..	..	..	..	..	..	..	..
5	II	..	..	..	..	..	..	..	x	x	x
6 *	II	x	..	x	..	x	x	x	..	x	self
7	I	..	..	..	..	..	x	x	..	self	x
8 *	I	..	..	..	..	..	..	..	..	..	..
9	I	..	..	..	..	..	..	..	..	..	..
10 *	III	..	x	..	x	x	x	..	..	x	x
11	II	..	..	x	..	x	x	x	..	..	x
12	II	..	x	..	..	..	..	..	..	..	..
13 *	II	..	x	x	..	x	x	x	..	x	x
14	II	..	..	x	..	..	..	..	..	..	x
15	I	..	..	x	x	x	x	x	x	x	x
16 *	II	..	..	..	..	..	x	..	..	..	x
17	I	x	..	x	..	..	x	x	..	x	..
18	II	x	..	..	..	..	x	x	..	x	..
19	I	..	..	..	..	..	..	x	x	..	x
20	II	..	..	..	..	..	..	x	..	..	..
21	I	..	..	..	x	..	..	..	..	..	..
22	I	..	..	..	..	..	..	..	..	..	x
23 *	I	x	..	..	..	x	x	x	..	..	x
24	II	..	..	..	..	..	self	x	..	x	x
25	I	..	..	..	..	..	..	x	..	..	..
26	II	x	..	..	..	x	x	x	x	x	x
27	II	x	..	..	..	x	x	..	..	..	x
28	II	x	x	x	x	x	x	x	..	x	x
29	I	..	..	..	x	x	..	..	x	..	x

TABLE 22—*Continued.*

Community leaders	Social class	Mrs. Reed	Wilson	Mason	Rogers	Mrs. Thomas	Hughes	Mrs. Parker	White	Thomas	Remington	
						Hospital board members						
30 *	I	x	..	..	..	x	x	wife	..	x	x	
31	III	..	..	..	..	..	..	..	..	..	..	
32	III	..	..	..	..	..	..	..	..	..	..	
33	II	..	..	..	..	x	x	x	..	x	..	
34	III	..	..	..	..	..	..	..	..	..	x	
35	III	..	..	..	..	..	..	..	..	..	..	
36	III	..	x	..	..	..	..	x	x	..	..	
37	II	x	..	..	..	x	x	x	x	x	x	
38	II	x	..	x	..	..	..	x	..	..	..	
39	III	..	..	..	..	..	x	x	x	..	x	
40	III	x	..	x	..	x	x	x	..	..	x	
41	I	..	..	x	x	..	..	..	..	..	..	
42	I	x	..	..	..	..	x	x	x	x	x	
43	I	..	..	..	..	..	..	..	..	..	..	
44	I	self	..	..	..	x	..	x	..	..	x	
45	I	..	..	..	..	..	..	..	x	..	x	
46	I	x	..	..	..	x	x	self	..	x	x	
47 *	I	x	..	..	..	x	x	x	..	x	x	
48 *	III	..	..	..	..	..	..	x	x	..	..	
49 *	II	..	..	..	..	..	..	..	..	..	..	
50 *	II	..	..	..	..	..	x	x	x	x	x	
51 *	II	x	x	..	..	x	x	x	x	x	x	
52 *	II	..	x	..	..	..	..	..	self	..	..	
Totals		16	7	10	6	20	23	27	15	18	29	171

* " Most nominated " influential.

† The total number of community leaders in this and the following table is higher than that in earlier tables because the leadership criteria used here included *formal membership* in boards or commissions associated with a given decision. This criterion was not used in the major part of the study.

each other. A considerable overlap of directorships in community organizations exists between board members and the most-nominated leaders, and within this leadership group itself. In sum, there is a socially homogeneous, integrated group of leaders in Edgewood who are, in turn, closely tied in with members of the hospital board.

The comparative lack of organizational associations between the Riverview hospital board and members of the power structure is accompanied by an even more marked paucity of close social ties between these two groups. As Table 23 shows, only thirty-six per cent of all Riverview leaders reported knowing any of the board members socially. The comparable proportion of Edgewood leaders who knew at least one board member socially was eighty-five per cent.

Even more striking is that these social acquaintances are almost completely limited to two members of the Riverview board, Richard Cavenaugh and Fred Rivers, two of the most-nominated influentials on the board. The third most-nominated leader on the board, Reverend Frank Baxter, is known socially by only three of the other community leaders. In addition, no community leaders acknowledge a close social acquaintance with two other board members, John Wolchak and Harold Plank. Nor can these differences between Edgewood and Riverview be explained completely in terms of differences in the social class composition of the power structure in the two communities. Regardless of class, leaders in Riverview are less likely to know any board member socially than are their counterparts in Edgewood.

Turning to a brief consideration of more direct types of involvement of community leaders in hospital affairs, there is, in one sense, little difference between the communities. Three board members in Riverview were also most-nominated influentials, while Edgewood has on its board only one such individual, R. G. White and the wife of another. Don Remington, another leader, is not a member of the board, although he attends its meetings regularly in an advisory capacity.

However, these similarities in direct participation of leaders in the hospital board mask some rather important differences in the roles they have played as board members in their respective communities. Richard Cavenaugh, president of the board in Riverview, has served on it for over twenty years. Son of one of the most prominent men of the past in the community, he is also president of the city's largest bank. In addition to being a most-nominated influential, he was active in three of the five major decisions, flood control, new industry, and hospital.

His participation in these decisions as well as his performance in meetings of the hospital board reveal several important characteristics of his leadership role. He was not an *initiator* of any decision. Even in the case of the establishment of the hospital authority, the main impetus came from the mayor, the city attorney, and the editor of the newspaper, who was at that time president of the Chamber of Commerce. As far as these three issues and the hospital are concerned, Cavenaugh's main contributions appear to be largely of a technical nature. As the city's leading banker and a member of the board of the federal reserve bank, he has access to financial institutions outside of the community. He is a man who knows money in the sense that he knows how to go about making financial arrangements.

TABLE 23 Social connections (exchange of home visits) between hospital board members and community leaders in Riverview

Community leaders	Social class	Wolchak	Plank	Schmidt	Mrs. King	Baxter	Rivers	Cavenaugh
1 *	IV	..	..	..	..	..	..	..
2	III	..	..	x	..	..	..	..
3	II	..	..	..	..	..	..	..
4	III	..	..	..	..	..	..	..
5	III	..	..	..	..	..	..	..
6 *	II	..	..	..	..	..	x	x
7	III	..	..	..	..	..	..	..
8	III	..	..	..	..	..	..	..
9 *	I	..	..	..	..	..	x	x
10	III	..	..	..	..	..	..	..
11 *	II	..	..	..	x	..	self	..
12 *	I	..	..	..	x	..	..	self
13 *	I	..	..	..	..	self	..	..
14	II	..	..	..	wife	..	x	x
15	II	..	..	..	..	..	..	..
16	I	..	..	..	..	..	x	x
17	III	..	..	..	..	..	..	..
18	II	..	..	..	..	..	x	x
19 *	I	..	..	..	..	..	..	..
20	III	self	..	..	..	..	..	..
21	II	..	..	..	..	..	..	..
22 *	III	..	..	..	..	..	x	x
23	III	..	..	..	..	..	..	..
24	II	..	..	..	..	..	..	..
25	I	..	..	x	..	..	x	x
26	II	..	self	..	..	..	..	..
27	IV	..	..	..	..	..	..	..
28	III	..	..	..	..	..	..	..
29	II	..	..	..	x	..	x	x
30	V	..	..	..	..	..	..	..
31	IV	..	..	..	..	..	..	..
32	III	..	..	..	..	..	..	..
33	IV	..	..	..	..	x	x	..
34	IV	..	..	..	..	..	..	..
35	II	..	..	..	..	..	..	..
36	II	..	..	..	..	..	..	..

TABLE 23—*Continued*

| | | Hospital board members | | | | | | |
Community leaders	Social class	Wolchak	Plank	Schmidt	Mrs. King	Baxter	Rivers	Cavenaugh
37	III	..	..	..	..	..	..	..
38	III	..	..	..	..	..	..	..
39	II	..	..	self	..	..	..	..
40	IV	..	..	..	..	..	..	..
41	I	..	..	..	..	x	x	x
42	II	..	..	..	..	..	..	..
43 *	II	..	..	..	x	..	x	x
44 *	II	..	..	..	x	x	x	x
45 *	II	..	..	..	x	..	x	..
46 *	III	..	..	x	..	..	..	..
47 *	I	..	..	..	..	..	..	..
Totals		0	0	3	6	3	13	11 36

* " Most nominated " influential.

Despite his personal wealth, his formal position in the community, and his long association with the hospital, he has apparently never made any real attempt to persuade others in the community to help the hospital financially. While he has made his technical knowledge available to both the hospital and the community, he has not used the influence inherent in his position in the community for the benefit of the local hospital. His conservatism and traditional way of doing things have sometimes inhibited innovation both in the community and in the hospital.

The Reverend Mr. Baxter, a newcomer to the Riverview board, has established himself solidly during the ten years he has lived in the community. A highly motivated, community-minded man, he was minimally involved in bringing the new industry to the community, and he also participated in the citizens' advisory committees for the new high school and the hospital. His main contribution to both the community and the hospital has been his skill as a manipulator of verbal and written symbols. He was chief publicist on the two citizens' committees in which he was active, and he has served for two years as chairman of the community relations committee of the hospital board. It was largely through his efforts that the local chapter of the Red Cross finally established a Gray Ladies unit (volunteer service) in the hospital in 1960.

Yet, his role was essentially ceremonial, as illustrated by an incident during one meeting of the hospital board. Before this meeting and in the ones that followed, he rarely participated in any way in the board's discussions. Furthermore, he was not often consulted by his colleagues on the board. As a member of the state social action committee of his church, as well as several other liberal organizations, his views are often inapposite to those of other board members. At the beginning of this particular meeting, a letter of resignation from the hospital administrator was read, and Dr. Baxter was asked if he would write a reply. During the meeting he composed a letter which he read to the board shortly before adjournment. The members listened in awed silence to his nice prose and well-turned phrases. In the process, Dr. Baxter talked longer than at any other time during the four board meetings covered in the research.

The third most-nominated member of the board, Fred Rivers, is a local contractor and business man who has served for a number of years on the school board and was active in the flood control decision. Prior to his appointment to the hospital board two years earlier, he had never had any connection with the hospital, and, like Cavenaugh, has never contributed any money or equipment to it. Commenting on the reasons for his appointment to the board, he observed:

> . . . The mayor came down to me around Christmas time and wanted me to resign from the school board so I could go on the hospital commission. I told him I would serve on both of them. A lot of people like to magnify the time they spend being on boards. That's what we have well-paid principals and superintendents for—to do the work. Anyway, there's no secret about it. The only reason they appointed me [to the hospital board] was because I was in construction work, and they felt better having someone like me around when they were building a new hospital.

Turning to leaders who are on the board of Edgewood Memorial, R. G. White, a recent appointee, is a vice president of one of the two banks in the community. White is a home-town boy who has worked his way up through various positions at the bank to his present post. At both the hospital and bank, he has taken the place of the same man. Before his appointment, his only involvement in the hospital was as a contributor and minor member of a fund-raising committee for the new hospital. During his time on the board, he has served as chairman of its finance committee and, in addition, handled most of the details involved in selecting and hiring a new administrator for the hospital. " In fact," the new administrator said later, " I hardly saw any of the other board members. All my arrangements and contacts were through Mr. White." In short, although he has been on the board for only one year, he appears to take a leading role in its affairs.

The man who receives most of the credit for the new hospital building and another decision-maker on the board is Don Remington. President of a locally-owned oil company, a director of GEI, and a member by marriage of one of the oldest families in Edgewood, Remington has access to the social and economic elite of the community. His role in the local power structure has been that of fund raiser. Besides being a member of the civic committee of the Rotary Club, which initiated the move for a new hospital, he organized and directed the drive which raised some $850,000 for the building. More recently, he was head of the drive to raise $100,000 to bring a new industry to Edgewood. As might be expected, he has great influence in board deliberations, especially where matters of money or relationships between the hospital and other community organizations are concerned.

Mrs. George Parker, one of the three women members of the board and wife of a most-nominated influential, is a representative of Edgewood " society." Her husband, a charming, cultured man, is legal counsel for one of the local banks, a member of its board of directors, and was chairman of the county Republican committee for over twenty-five years. Like other women members, she devotes a good deal of her time to church and hospital activities, and, in fact, their presence at board meetings frequently gives the meetings the atmosphere of a ladies' sewing circle. Considerable time is spent discussing the need for chintz curtains in the nurses' dressing room or the dustiness of closets. For this reason, most of the key decisions are made and carried out on an informal basis by White,

Remington, and George Wilson, another board member and a representative of Main Street business interests.

In addition to their board membership, there are a number of other ways in which decision-makers in the two communities could have played some direct part in hospital affairs. They could, of course, have given money to the hospital or have been members of volunteer groups which have done work for the hospitals. Our research indicates that community leaders in Edgewood are much more likely to have been directly involved in such activities than those in Riverview. Almost all such leaders reported making a voluntary contribution to the hospital at some time, while less than half of those in Riverview have done so. Leaders in Edgewood are considerably more likely to have given some of their time to hospital affairs than their counterparts in Riverview. Even when such factors as social class, family background, income, and length of residence are controlled, Edgewood leaders make a much better showing in these respects. In short, relationships between the hospital and the leadership structure in Edgewood have been much closer and more widespread, and the decision-makers as a group have been more likely to take an active interest than has been true in Riverview.

Support Theory Research and the Behavioral Approach

This example of organizational research illustrates several aspects of the behavioral approach. It is set in an explicit theoretical framework, which has been established as being useful for an understanding of an organization's capability in its larger social environment.[4] (This framework, by the way, is helpful for teaching purposes, providing a functional way of looking at an organization in which the implications of its interaction with its external environment become explicit).

The research is also highly self-conscious methodologically. Most disinterested men would probably agree that different levels of support had been shown to characterize the two hospitals. Quantitative, public indexes of such differences are presented. Finally, differences are shown in the extent to which board members and members of the power structure share organizational and social interaction. Sociometric analysis reveals a particularly dramatic variation in the latter sphere. Only thirty-six per cent of all Riverview leaders reported knowing any board members socially, compared with fully eighty-five per cent in Edgewood.

Here again, certain indicators are assumed to be valid indexes of the basic relationship we seek to understand. This common property of behavioral research puts one at second-remove from the phenomenon he is ultimately concerned with. In F-scale (authoritarianism) research, for example, responses to certain items (for example, " no decent man can respect a woman who has sexual relations before marriage ") are used as indicators of authoritarianism. In the present instance, organizational effectiveness is the prime concern. On a logical and theoretical basis, joint organizational memberships and social interactions (measured through home visits) are assumed to be valid operational criteria for behavior through which influence can be exerted and community resources tapped. Skeptics could, of course, argue that social relations are idiosyncratic and, in any case, are used only to further purely social ends. In effect, since the indicators are inadequate, any conclusions drawn from their use are invalid.

Perhaps the researcher would defend his work by citing earlier research demonstrating that personal interactions did indeed have extra-social implications. If he were a traditional scholar, he would probably point to historical instances of the influence wielded over certain kings and prime ministers by courtesans such as Madame DuBarry or éminences grises such as Rasputin. If he were a political scientist, he might cite research on personal influence showing that whom one votes for and his position on current issues are often determined by prestigeful individuals with whom he shares interpersonal contacts.[5] If he were an industrial sociologist, he would probably cite Elton Mayo's classic research in which group (social) influences on individual behavior and productivity were clearly demonstrated.[6]

Perhaps all this is only another way of saying that the significance of a problem is easier to establish than the relevance and validity of the instruments designed to research it. Certainly, it is easier to work conceptually at the level of grand theory than at a research-oriented level where specification and operationalization become necessary. One can talk rather freely about power and pluralism as philosophical or analytical categories, but as soon as one attempts to reduce them to testable propositions, his fluency generally decreases rapidly. This, of course, is true with respect to all the great, abstract nouns of our time, including "freedom," "democracy," "liberalism," and "conservatism." It is a rewarding and sobering experience to explicate these staples of our political diet.

4

Behavioral Research
on British Executives

WE NOW TURN TO SOME RECENT RESEARCH
to illustrate further the behavioral approach in public
administration. For some time I have been interested in
applying sociological and psychological concepts to behavior in large, bureaucratic organizations. Sociology, of
course, focuses on the nature and the influence of social
structure. It is essentially *environmental*, believing that
behavior is shaped mainly by the web of social values into
which the individual is born. In some large measure,
man is taught to honor ongoing norms by a process called
socialization. Socially-accepted and functionally-necessary
behavior is rewarded, while aberrant behavior is sanc-
tioned by tactics ranging from the mother's gentle repri-
mand to the judge's prison sentence.

Obviously, such an analytical thrust is immensely valua-
able and explains most of the behavior we see around us,
especially if it adequately accounts for the deviant behavior and normative conflicts that characterize any given
culture. Sociology often concerns itself with such themes,
and much of its early history was bound up with studies

of prejudice, juvenile delinquency, and crime. Indeed, perhaps more than economics, sociology has been the "dismal science." Nevertheless, while sociology uses deviant behavior as an instrument to illumine conventional styles of accommodation, deviation cannot be adequately explained by sociological formulations.* Psychological analysis, it appears, is also necessary. As a result I have tried to combine both approaches, using an essentially sociological approach to the structural, collective side (including, of course, both hierarchical roles and values) of organizational life and a psychological approach to explain the fact that hierarchical roles are obviously affected by personality.[1] The organization's attempts to socialize its members evoke discrete patterns of accommodation, and these variations can only be explained by differing individual perceptions of and reactions to the bureaucratic situation.

Cultural definitions of major social roles remain fairly stable, but individuals accommodate to such roles somewhat differently. Even a cursory look at presidential styles during our own lifetime validates this judgment. It seems to me that a major factor mediating such varying accommodations is an individual's attitudes toward authority, with anxiety playing a significant role. Since anxiety is a painful experience, we may assume that individuals attempt to reduce it by deferring to authority figures. It is well known that the approval of people who are significant to us has this reinforcing effect.

Authority is defined here as the capacity to evoke com-

* Perhaps "deviation" is too strong a term. I am thinking of *variations* in behavior that presumably would not occur if the socialization process operated perfectly.

pliance on the basis of one's formal status and of any psychological inducements, rewards, or sanctions that may accompany formal position. Authority in truth has several bases of legitimation, including formal role or status, expertise, rapport or empathy, and a residual category consisting of a generalized deference to authority instilled in the individual from birth onward through the socialization process. In any given situation, one or another of these legitimations may be decisive, depending upon the preferences and expectations of those involved.

In the research reported here, authority is operationalized along three dimensions: the executive's desire for independence in his authority relations with immediate superiors; the extent to which he legitimates his organizations right to expect certain modes of behavior on and off the job; and finally, his attitudes toward authority as measured in terms of selected authoritarian (F-scale) values. In effect, authority is conceptualized at several levels, ranging from a specific, job-related context, through an area of organizational expectations, to the generalized level of personality. The use of these discrete, yet theoretically related, dimensions should enable us to categorize the executives in terms of their reactions to authority and to determine how such categories are related to career success.

The ability to handle authority gracefully is assumed to be critical in organizations because they are essentially, as C. Wright Mills has said, " systems of hierarchical roles graded by authority." Perhaps the major currency in the bureaucratic interpersonal market, authority may rest upon skill, seniority, status, or empathy, or some combination of these. Any given actor must interact daily with subordinates, superiors, and equals; the behavioral dynamics of each situation differ. This demands a certain versatility, not only in a superficial " professional mask " context, but in a deeper sense which engages personality, that is, one's learned ways of handling interpersonal situations.

Now, it seems that most of us can handle interpersonal relations in organizations fairly well. Among the highly trained professionals increasingly found in organizations, sensitivity to the rational bases of authority, to the " law of the situation," reduces the tensions inherent in authority relations in our free-and-easy society. Yet, at higher levels where an individual must deal with many varied and complex authority situations, problems seem to increase geometrically. Individuals who can play a graceful and controlled authority role only by violating their basic personal needs must, it follows, experience considerable tension in such roles. Indeed, I do not believe that any executive can long play such a role if it is contrary to his personality structure. He will gradually adopt stereotyped authority relations that are natural to him. (In Platonic terms, insofar as justice requires that each individual be treated differently, giving to each his due, he will also sacrifice justice, because his style of accommodation prevents such nice discriminations.) This accommodation may be conscious, or it may be subconscious, in the sense that he is obliged to adopt it even though it complicates his authority relations.

A further hypothesis is that the bases of such accommodations are mainly acquired in childhood. (One can, I believe, offer such a proposition without denying that personality change occurs throughout an individual's life.) Studies of child-raising behavior show that middle-class and working-class parents instill in their children quite different attitudes and methods of handling authority.[2] Briefly, whereas working-class children are often encouraged to aggress against authority, middle-class parents teach their children to handle it by more rational, less explosive methods. They are taught to turn aggression inward, to ask whether their frustrations are not in part the result of their own behavior. This accommodation is likely to be rewarding because it permits learning.

These different patterns of socialization are begun by parents who handle their own authority relations vis-à-vis their own children in such different ways. They are reinforced by subsequent experiences with other authority figures. This formulation, based mainly on the empirical work of Harry Stack Sullivan,[3] suggests a link between social class, perceptions of authority, and organizational success. Evidence showing a positive association between class and organizational mobility is plentiful, and it seems that further specification of the relationship might be obtained by research in this theoretical framework.

An opportunity occurred last year for me to test some of these propositions, using a sample of British executives in two large corporations, British European Airways (BEA) and British Industrials, Ltd. (BIL).* Some preliminary analysis of the findings throws some light on the question of role accommodation in large bureaucratic structures. Moreover, since one never puts all his research eggs in one basket, the design included other aspects of organizational behavior such as relations between career

* I am indebted to the Social Science Research Council for the grant which supported this research.

success and attitudes toward work, personal qualities associated with mobility, and so on. Some of these findings will be reported.

Finally, the usual data on class, politics, religion, income, and ethnicity were secured, and these make possible interesting comparative analysis. My use of the term "usual" requires a comment on what might be called cultural differences affecting research. It is still something less than usual to secure data on politics, income, and religion among British respondents, because survey research is not yet widely accepted in England. As a result, I encountered some resistance in gaining access to organizations and once inside, found a certain amount of reluctance on the part of some individuals who apparently participated mainly because they felt that the research had been authorized by the highest levels of management.

Obviously, I am speaking in terms of degree here, since the fact that the research was completed indicates that a large measure of co-operation was received. However, broadly speaking, it was more difficult to gain access and carry out the research than expected on the basis of similar experience in the United States. For example, even though I approached eight major corporations, and had fairly good sponsorship, I gained access into only two firms. Partly, no doubt, this was because my research was of an attitudinal kind which could not promise any useful results in exchange for the time required on the corporation's part. Yet, my own conclusion is that the main problem was one of opposition to the principle of such research, which runs against dominant British themes of amateurism, humanism, and resistance to the values associated with American industrial research and management practices.[4] Another factor was the understandable reluctance of the executives to reveal to an outsider their private views and group affiliations. (I am quite sure that this reluctance is also related to conditions of life on a very crowded island where privacy can only be insured by systematic and symbolic effort, which includes building walls around every yard, a great deal of reserve in interpersonal relations, the emphasis upon private clubs, schools, and the like. It may be that these behaviors are inspired less by social class considerations, as often assumed, than by the simple effort to retain privacy.) Indeed, I am convinced that I was able to secure data on religion, income, and political affiliations only because the executives concluded that, being a foreigner, I just didn't understand that one doesn't ask such questions, and that perhaps it would do no great harm to humor me.

In any event, items designed to test attitudes toward authority were included in the questionnaire, including several from the Adorno F-scale.[5] My hypothesis was that a positive association existed between career success and the acceptance of organizational authority. Specifically, men who experienced most success seemed more likely than others to accept the organization's claims for loyalty, consistency, and obedience; to believe more strongly that the rewards accruing to those who have most authority were legitimate; and in general to endorse more positively F-scale values that honor status differentiations, conventionality, the need for leaders to be strict, and the benefits of hard work.

Another set of items differentiated the executives in terms of the limits they placed on the organization's right to influence certain kinds of extra-job behavior of its members. Did they believe, for example, that it was proper for the organization to be concerned whether or not they used its products? Such evidence would reveal authority perspectives along a related, but conceptually different, dimension. (Here again, the importance of the cultural environment of research was seen. I found that most British executives were not sensitized to the " organization-man " ethic which underlay these items. On the one hand, this reduced the comparative utility of the data, but on the other, it meant that they would be less likely to bend their responses in an effort to demonstrate their sophistication regarding this aspect of organizational life.) Individuals who put few limits on such organizational demands would, it seemed, be less likely to have difficulty in handling authority in a bureaucratic context; would be more likely to identify closely with the organization than their more independent colleagues; and henceforth, more likely to have been highly successful. Finally, insofar as acceptance of the organization's expectations reflects an individual's identification with dominant social values, it also seemed that an alienation scale might separate highly-mobile from less-mobile respondents.

Although the concept of authoritarianism is obviously broader than the concept of bureaucratic authority, the two are related. It has been found, for example, that executives who rank high on authoritarianism are more likely to endorse the authority of their superiors.[6] They seem more likely to be able to accept decisions from above without strain, in part because they accept the existing distribution of authority and status. They are more likely to feel that they can control events.

Some of the conditions of success in big organizations

thus seem related to some of the values typically ascribed to the so-called authoritarian personality. These generally include considerable sensitivity to status and power differentials, the desire for consistent, well-ordered interpersonal relations, the belief that businessmen and industrialists are more important to society than the artist or the intellectual, and a general preference for disciplined, conventional, status-prescribed behavior. If this assumption

TABLE 24   Organizational mobility and authoritarianism *

| | | Mobility | |
Authoritarianism	High (138)	Medium (109)	Low (161)
High	57%	54%	44%

* Authoritarianism is measured by a scale comprising the following items: " People should be more careful with their money and save it instead of spending it all "; " No decent man can respect a woman who has had sex relations before marriage "; " We should fight an all-out war to stop world communism before it gets any stronger than it is." The scale, which has a reproducibility of .90, was coded as follows: low, 0 affirmative responses; medium, 1, 2 affirmative responses; high, 3 affirmative responses.

is valid, highly successful executives should rank somewhat higher on certain F-scale items than those who have been less successful in the bureaucratic arena. Table 24 compares highly-mobile and less-mobile executives in these terms.

Although the differences are not always statistically significant, the data generally support the hypothesis. Executives who have experienced the greatest organizational mobility also rank highest on authoritarianism (fifty-seven per cent). There is, moreover, a significant difference

between them and the least successful executives ranking
high on authoritarianism (forty-four per cent). This positive relation suggests that some of the values typically
associated with authoritarianism are indeed functional in
large-scale organizations. The finding, in effect, supports
one of the main theoretical propositions of *The Organizational Society,* which held that the upward-mobile types
who found the bureaucratic situation congenial would be
likely to possess certain authoritarian values including
conventionality, aggressiveness, respect for power and authority, personal discipline, and so on. The relationship
is impressive when one considers that highly successful
executives are disproportionately recruited from upper-
class and upper-middle-class groups, members of which
have usually been found to rank low on authoritarianism
compared with those from other class strata.

Attitudes toward authority were next analyzed along
the dimension of organizational expectations, using the
following indicators: " I believe it is proper for my organization to be concerned with, 1) whether or not I use
its products, 2) my own attitude toward sexual morality,
3) the tidiness of my office, 4) the number of drinks (if
any) I have at lunch." The rationale here is that responses will indicate the extent to which an executive
legitimates the authority of the organization in a highly
generalized context. Thus a high level of acceptance can
be regarded as a valid indicator of a generally positive
attitude toward organizational authority.

A difficulty here, pointed out by some respondents, is
that such items are not always perceived in an authority
context, but instead they may be viewed as expressions

of a perfectly normal loyalty to an organization in which one has chosen to spend a good deal of his life. British conceptions of work and the work-place do indeed stress loyalty and long service to a greater extent than in the United States. The philosophy is similar to that reported of Japan, where the employer apparently assumes a protective, familial relationship with his employees rather than the strictly contractual nexus often found in our society. On the other hand, it does seem that loyalty to the organization is very much like our conception of authority as a positive acceptance of the organization's policies.

Affirmative responses were simply totaled, ranging from " low," (no affirmative answers) to " high " (affirmative on all four items). The resulting associations are shown in Table 25.

TABLE 25   Organizational mobility and acceptance of organizational authority

| Acceptance | Mobility | |
	High (138)	Low (272)
High	34%	39%

Contrary to our hypothesis that acceptance would be higher among those who had experienced the greatest job success, less successful executives proved somewhat more willing to accept the organization's influence in matters that seem marginal insofar as their job performance is concerned. Findings such as these inspired Carl Rogers' comment regarding frustrated hypotheses: " The facts are always friendly." In effect, one should not be disenchanted by an unverified hypothesis, but should regard it as a step on the way to valid generalizations. In his view, this is part of the necessary waste in research work.

In any event, from this evidence, one must conclude tentatively that less-successful members of an organization tend to be more subject to these latent kinds of organizational expectations. One can only speculate as to the reasons. Small-group research indicates that high-status members of a group are granted a great deal more latitude regarding group expectations and rules than their less prestigious brethren.[7] Yet, at the same time, other research finds that leaders tend to reflect group norms more faithfully than other members. Such differences probably rest in the peculiar function and structure of the group tested.

Given the British executives' apparent lack of familiarity with current organization-man themes in the United States, it is interesting to compare their responses on four of these items with an American sample. Table 26 gives the distributions.

Along a scale ranging from plus one-hundred to minus one-hundred, the relative scale position of each item is similar in both groups. In effect, their zone of indifference on these discrete manifestations of organizational authority is similar. In each case, however, the British executives are far less willing to grant the organization's right to influence their behavior. Had they been sensitized to the organization-man theme, the differences would probably have been even greater.

Thus, it is apparent that mobility is not positively related to acceptance when authority is defined by highly generalized organizational expectations. Another more specific dimension was then analyzed, namely, relationships with superiors. Respondents were given items designed to distribute them along a continuum ranging from a strong desire for personal independence in hierarchical

TABLE 26 Comparative executive attitudes on selected authority variables

	American (391) *	British (409)
"I believe it is proper for my organization to be concerned with the tidiness of my office."	88 †	53
"I believe it is proper for my organization to be concerned with how many drinks (if any) I have at lunch."	77	28
"I believe it is proper for my organization to be concerned about whether or not I use its products."	21	1.5
"I believe it is proper for my organization to be concerned with my own attitude toward sexual morality."	15	−68

* The American data are from E. H. Schein and J. S. Ott, " The Legitimacy of Organizational Influence," 47 *American Journal of Sociology* (May, 1962), p. 685.

† The results here are given in terms of averaged index numbers, composed of " no " minus " yes " responses multiplied by 100. The possible range is from +100 to −100, with +100 indicating maximum agreement. However, comparability is clouded by the fact that the American items included a " no answer " category, while the British items permitted only " yes " or " no " responses. The effect of this difference is unknown, although it is not assumed to be great.

relationships to one of extreme dependency upon their superiors. The association shown in Table 27 appeared.

Here again, although the facts may be friendly, they do not support the theory. Instead, a positive association is found between job success and the desire for independence insofar as relations with superiors are concerned. This suggests that successful executives handle their authority relations differently than their less-mobile counterparts. They are apparently more likely to oppose higher

TABLE 27   Organizational mobility and the desire for independence *

| | Mobility | | |
Independence	High (138)	Medium (109)	Low (161)
High	54%	50%	44%

* The following items were used: " Assume that your immediate superior, after consultation, during which you indicated your opposition, went ahead with an important decision that you strongly believed was wrong from the standpoint of the interests of the organization. Which of the following alternatives would you follow? a) Try quietly to undercut the decision through ' passive resistance '; b) Attempt to convince a high executive who could countermand the decision; c) Resign as a protest; d) Keep still and carry out the decision as well as possible."

"Concerning my relations with superiors, I generally prefer a work situation in which: a) Supervision is fairly close so as to minimize costly errors; b) My ' boss ' works right along with me as the programme or policy develops; c) In general, I can share the responsibility for a decision with those above me; d) I am given a general objective and left completely alone to carry it out."

authority and to want complete freedom in carrying out their assignments. This finding, of course, conforms nicely to the conventional image of the successful executive who welcomes responsibility and makes the most of his authority. The linear relationship across the three mobility levels suggests that we have found a variable that differentiates successful and less-successful executives.

One other approach to organizational authority can be made, based on the theoretical assumption that a complex organization is a miniature society, governed by the same major values that operate in the larger system. Organizations, in a word, are systems in which individuals strive to attain desired social values, including prestige, income, and security. If status anxiety, for example, is a major characteristic of our society, we should find it similarly compelling in any given work organization. In this context, it seems that alienation might be a useful construct to analyze executive attitudes toward authority. If an individual rejects authoritative social values, it seems that he might also deny the legitimacy of organizational norms and expectations. If he believes himself to be ineffectual in community and national politics, this attitude should also characterize his perceptions of his influence in an organizational context. If he regards loyalty to a group or a political party as a mark of naïveté, he might regard the organization's more or less obvious expectations of loyalty as naïve. We thus assume that alienation provides an indicator of attitudes toward organizational authority.

Using a four-item alienation scale, I found the association shown in Table 28.

Here the data strongly support the hypothesis. Alienation is inversely related to the acceptance of organizational authority. The highest proportion of highly alienated executives, thirty-eight per cent, is found among those who rank lowest on acceptance of authority, and this proportion is exactly twice as high as that found for executives ranking high on this dimension.

These findings suggest a relation between low alienation and career success, if we assume that success is associated with acceptance of the organization's expectations. Here again, as Table 29 shows, the association is positive.

TABLE 28   Acceptance of organizational authority and alienation *

| Alienation | Acceptance of authority | | |
	High (153)	Medium (134)	Low (116)
High	19%	29%	38%

* This scale is composed of the following items: "a) Most people are inclined to look out for themselves; b) Most decisions in organizations are made by a small group that pretty well runs things; c) Nowadays a person has to live pretty much for today and let tomorrow take care of itself; d) It is hardly fair to bring children into the world the way things look for the future." This scale's reproducibility is .89. Responses were coded as follows: low, 0-1 affirmative responses; medium, 2-3 affirmative responses; high, 4 affirmative responses.

TABLE 29   Organizational mobility and alienation

| Alienation | Mobility | | |
	High (138)	Medium (109)	Low (161)
High	6%	12%	10%

Although the relationship is not linear, the data show the expected relationship between mobility and alienation. In both corporations, men who have attained the highest rank are less alienated than other executives. Since alienation includes feelings of personal inefficacy regarding one's ability to influence events, one would expect these men to rank low on this variable. Their successful careers remind them daily that they have achieved a great deal, and their job responsibilities enable them to exert considerable influence over men and events in their own organizations, and, presumably, in the political life of their communities.

It will be recalled that our theory of accommodation posited anxiety as a critical mediating factor in reactions to organizational authority. The initial belief was that a tendency to defer to the authority of superiors would characterize successful executives. In part, this assump-

TABLE 30   Organizational mobility and anxiety *

| Anxiety | Mobility | | |
	High (138)	Medium (109)	Low (161)
High	15%	20%	50%

* An abbreviated version of the Taylor Manifest Anxiety scale was used. A correlation of .90 has been found between the 31 items used and the original 50-item scale. J. A. Taylor, " A Personality Scale of Manifest Anxiety," 48 *Journal of Social and Abnormal Psychology* (1953), pp. 285-90.

tion was based upon the research of Gardner, Warner, and Henry who had found both this tendency and considerable anxiety (fear of failure) among highly successful executives.[8] An anxiety scale was included in the questionnaire in order to test for any significant associations in this context. Following Sullivan, the main assumption here was that since anxiety-reduction is a compelling motivation, and since deferring to the authority of significant others is a major way of reducing anxiety, a positive association between high mobility and anxiety might be found.

Here again, the data failed to sustain the hypothesis. Indeed, as Table 30 indicates, anxiety is inversely asso-

ciated with mobility. This table includes all those ranking high on anxiety, a group comprising only ten per cent
of the entire sample. As the data show, fully half of these
men are in the lowest mobility category. This inverse
relation between success and anxiety probably reflects
other factors such as class, education, and income. In
order to specify one of these intervening variables, we
ran anxiety against class, with the results shown in
Table 31.

TABLE 31   Class status and anxiety

Class status	High anxiety
I (25)	2%
II (95)	24
III (196)	58
IV (48)	16

Although the relationship is curvilinear, anxiety and
class are inversely associated. We assume that the higher
education, income, and prestige enjoyed by the small
upper-class group explains their very low ranking on
anxiety. They possess more highly-valued resources and
thus more psychic security. The larger social context of
this judgment includes the common public school background of these men, which carefully instills in them the
belief that they are destined for leadership. Although
only a few of them go on to Oxbridge, when they do, this
self-image is again reinforced. We can only speculate
about the unexpected difference between the III and IV
levels. Perhaps those in the lowest status have resigned
themselves to their limited mobility and are no longer,
in the delightful British term, " thrusters."

Broadly speaking, anxiety is probably less pervasive in British society than in American. Not only is there a tradition and an expectation that a man will remain in a single organization during most of his work life, but there is probably somewhat less class and career mobility.* Given man's capacity for rationalization, the results may include a tendency for individuals to regard both their work and their work-place more favorably. Relaxed resignation may follow. One bit of supporting evidence appeared when we found that British executives were much less likely than their American counterparts to endorse the statement that people no longer work hard enough (see p. 129). This may suggest less acceptance of the Protestant ethic honoring work, personal discipline, accumulation, and so on. Again, job satisfaction among the British sample is generally high (see p. 144), and long service in both corporations is very common.

One of the strongest relationships found in this preliminary analysis is between organizational mobility and political conservatism. The stability, consistency, and respect for established authority that characterize political conservatives are apparently well-suited to the bureaucratic situation. Organizations of most kinds, including universities, one suspects, prefer steady men who will fit into the ongoing web of custom, power, and authority. Most organizations, moreover, spend most of their time carrying out rather stereotyped activities, which seldom

* Some researchers have concluded that social mobility rates are similar in the United States and Western Europe, but given the startlingly unequal opportunity in Britain for university education, which is today the major instrument of mobility, such evidence must be questioned.

require, and indeed are inapposite to, individuals who retain some spontaneity and the belief that change is the law of life. Organizations, in effect, require Stalins rather than Lenins, for their role is usually to make good some past revolution. It is not surprising, therefore, to find a strong positive association between conservatism and bureaucratic success, as shown in Table 32. Of those who are high on organizational mobility, thirty-seven per cent

TABLE 32   Organizational mobility and political conservatism *

	Mobility		
Conservatism	High (138)	Medium (109)	Low (161)
High	37%	28%	22%

* Political conservatism was measured by a scale comprising the following items: "Democracy depends fundamentally on the existence of free enterprise"; "We have moved too far away from those fundamental principles that made England great"; "An atheist or communist should have as much right as anyone else to make a public speech in London" (reverse scored). Reproducibility of this scale was .94.

are high on conservatism, a level which declines significantly as one moves across the lower levels of mobility.

Although not shown here, a noteworthy difference between the two samples exists at the very highest level of mobility where the proportion of British Industrials' executives ranking high on conservatism was fully one-third larger than in BEA. Since BEA is a government-owned corporation, while BIL is private, this difference is probably not surprising.

The relation of organizational mobility to job satisfaction was our next concern. A positive association between these variables would be expected, but it is known that many members of large organizations are not highly motivated toward promotion since, along with its rewards come more responsibility and more demands for complete involvement in one's work. Insofar as such individuals find job satisfaction in other aspects of their work, the anticipated association might not appear.

Job satisfaction was measured by four items, beginning with a straight-forward question asking respondents to indicate their position on a high-medium-low scale. In addition, three indirect indicators were used: whether

TABLE 33   Organizational mobility and job satisfaction

| | Mobility | | |
Job satisfaction	High (138)	Medium (109)	Low (161)
High	73%	61%	55%

(if they had the choice) they would choose the same career again; whether they found their job generally suitable to their skill and experience; and whether they would recommend their kind of work to a young friend of the family. The associations found appear in Table 33.

This positive association indicates that career success is a major determinant of job satisfaction among these executives. In line with earlier research showing that job satisfaction rises steadily from blue-collar through white-collar to executive-professional statuses, the general level of satisfaction among these men is high. Less than one per cent of them marked the low category, while only forty per cent indicated even a medium level of satisfaction. As noted earlier, the British tradition of long service in a single organization is probably at work here, as well as the bureaucratic standardization that characterizes large-scale organizations in Western society. I was told by one personnel director, for example, that a half-dozen giants, including British Petroleum, English Electric, Imperial Chemicals, Shell, and Unilever, meet periodically to synchronize conditions of work and pay for their executive jobs. If pay, pensions, and perquisites are similar in large organizations and for a given variety of specialists regardless of their work-place, invidious comparisons are obviously less likely to occur.

The relationship between mobility and class status is our next concern. American research has demonstrated that social class, usually based upon father's occupation and respondent's education, is strongly associated with success in American industry. Newcomer, for example, found that some 600 high-level executives in major corporations had nine times the amount of education possessed by American men in their own age category. They were mainly from middle-class and upper-middle-class families who enjoyed incomes well above the average.[9] A similar relationship among our British sample was anticipated.

Class status is indeed related to mobility, as Table 34 shows. Representation in the high mobility category rises steadily with class. Executives of upper-class tsatus, for example, are greatly overrepresented among the most successful group. Only six per cent (N = 25) of the entire sample is of upper-class origin, yet they provide over half of the top group. On the other hand, lower-middle-class executives (class IV), who provide about twelve per cent of the entire group, are unrepresented in the high category.

TABLE 34 Organizational mobility and class status *

Class status	High mobility
I (25)	52%
II (95)	35
III (196)	12
IV (48)	0

* Class status is determined by three weighted variables: father's occupation, respondent's education, and respondent's income. Since all these men are managers, their own occupation is constant. Roughly, the four class categories are defined as follows: I, upper; II, upper-middle; III, middle-middle; IV, lower-middle.

The superior mobility of favored class groups is related to their attitudes toward authority, as suggested by Table 35.

TABLE 35 Class status and authority preferences

Class status	Prefer independence
I (25)	61%
II (95)	51
III (196)	49
IV (48)	42

We saw earlier that mobility was positively related to a desire for independence in supervisory relations and a willingness to resist higher authority in extreme cases. It seems that upper-class executives possess more of these qualities than their less-favored colleagues. At the same time, of course, their preferred class status reflects a higher level of educational achievement, which also underlies their greater mobility.

Our findings may be summarized by a comparison of various properties in terms of their mobility value. See Table 36.

TABLE 36   Comparative utility of selected mobility properties

Property	Useful	Less useful
Attitude to authority	Independent	Dependent
Authoritarianism	High	Low
Anxiety	Low	High
Alienation	Low	High
Political conservatism	High	Low
Social class	Upper and upper-middle	Middle and lower-middle

Some American-British Comparisons

Having considered some preliminary findings from the British sample, it seems useful to compare them with an American sample of managers. The latter are from the New York community study, and include some 200 respondents with a manager occupational classification. Two characteristics of this sample should be noted: unlike the British group, almost all of whom work in large corporations in London, this is a random group of managers in both large and small organizations located in two small communities. We don't know exactly what the effects of these differences are. One might argue that standardized mass media and consumption styles in the United States and Britain tend to wash away any urban-rural differences, so that the important variable is over-all, national differences in basic cultural values. I think this rationale is valid. On the other hand, small-town people may have characteristic attitudes about political affairs; perhaps

Gemeinschaft relationships in small communities make for less political cynicism, greater tolerance, more acceptance of big government, and the like. This question cannot be resolved here, but should be kept in mind when evaluating the findings.

Because comparable authoritarianism, alienation, and conservatism scales could not be produced for both the American (N = 207) and British (N = 409) samples, we are obliged to compare the two groups on individual items. With only two or three exceptions, only those in which significant differences appear will be reported here. We begin with several typical *authoritarianism* items.

"A good leader should be strict with people under him in order to gain their respect."

	Agree
United States	18%
Great Britain	43

"The most important thing to teach children is complete obedience to their parents."

	Agree
United States	60%
Great Britain	30

"There are two kinds of people in the world: the weak and the strong."

	Agree
United States	52%
Great Britain	27

"No decent man can respect a woman who has had sex relations before marriage."

	Agree
United States	27%
Great Britain	13

Even though these items are not scaled, it is noteworthy that the American managers score significantly
more authoritarian than the British on three of the four
items. They seem to feel more strongly about the need
for obedience, discipline, and conformity to conventional
norms, all of which are characteristic of the so-called
authoritarian personality. Nevertheless on the first item,
which is probably the most directly germane for bureaucratic relations, the British executives are substantially
more authoritarian. Certainly, leadership tends to have
more elitist implications in Britain than it has in the
United States, a fact about which Britain's feudal past and
its pervasive class sensitivity is capable of telling us a
great deal.

When political conservatism is analyzed, a similar difference between the two groups appears.

"An atheist or a communist (socialist *) should have as
much right as anyone else to make a public speech in
London (Edgewood, Riverview)."

	Agree
United States	70%
Great Britain	93

"On the whole, labor unions are doing a lot of good in this
country."

	Agree
United States	60%
Great Britain	82

* The term "socialist" had to be changed to "communist" for
the British sample, which suggests the difference in the political
complexions of the two countries.

" That government which governs least governs best."

	Agree
United States	92%
Great Britain	25

" We should give more of our foreign aid for social welfare types of projects."

	Agree
United States	66%
Great Britain	75

" One of the biggest problems with the world today is that people don't work hard enough anymore."

	Agree
United States	47%
Great Britain	33

" Democracy depends fundamentally on the existence of free enterprise."

	Agree
United States	91%
Great Britain	67

" England (U.S.) should be less concerned about what other countries think of her."

	Agree
United States	67%
Great Britain	51

Here is dramatic evidence of a significantly larger measure of political liberalism on the part of the British managers. American executives as a group tend to be much more conservative on matters involving government's role in society, internationalism, and the assumed relation between free markets and free men. Given the greater age of British society and its tradition of strong government, this general attitude is not surprising. The difference is all the more impressive when one notes that sixty-five per cent of the British managers are members of the Conservative Party. This underscores the well-known fact that British political opinion is considerably to the left of American, regardless of party affiliations.

Finally, to suggest further differences between the two groups, we present their comparative positions on several alienation items that measure their acceptance of such values as social mobility, sense of political effectiveness, opportunity to influence the voluntary groups to which they belong, and so on. Individuals who feel deprived or ineffectual in these areas are likely to score high on alienation.

"There is a lot of truth in the statement that 'nice guys finish last.'"

	Agree
United States	21%
Great Britain	41

"Life as most men live it is meaningless."

	Agree
United States	21%
Great Britain	24

"The average man doesn't really have much chance to get ahead today."

	Agree
United States	24%
Great Britain	22

" Most people are inclined to look out for themselves."

	Agree
United States	90%
Great Britain	90

In every case, the British managers are either equally or somewhat more likely to have an alienated view of human nature and individual opportunity. The belief that one has to be ruthless in order to succeed is, as indicated, considerably more widespread among British managers. This jaundiced view is in sharp contrast to their tendency to believe in political solutions and in their ability to influence government. The latter is probably one part of a general pro-government syndrome based upon common ethnic origins and cultural traditions which find expression in a larger role for British government. No doubt, too, the relative freedom of British government from the spoils system and other forms of political corruption sometimes present in the United States influences this attitude, as the next three items seem to emphasize.

" The old saying, ' You can't fight City Hall is still basically true.' "

	Agree
United States	70%
Great Britain	48

" On the whole, British (U.S.) participation in the United Nations has been a good thing."

	Agree
United States	77%
Great Britain	90

" The only hope for a real lasting peace is to establish some kind of world government."

	Agree
United States	27%
Great Britain	60

The last two items, which favor the use of political institutions to solve major problems, show that a substantially larger proportion of British respondents have faith in internatioal political organizations as the only hope for a lasting peace. Moreover, since our American sample is from New York state which is traditionally internationalist, these are probably the highest affirmative responses to be found in the United States. Certainly, opinions in Illinois or California would be less affirmative.

These responses suggest that the two samples are quite similar about some facets of alienation, such as the belief that the average man has a difficult time achieving success or that people generally look out for themselves. On the other hand, in matters concerning political or governmental themes, British managers tend to be significantly less alienated than their American counterparts. They believe in world government, in their capacity to influence city hall, and in strong government as opposed to weak. It is interesting to find, moreover, that there is no difference in this regard between executives in the private corporation, British Industrials, Ltd. and British European Airways, which is a public organization. Such political attitudes are apparently shaped by factors other than one's work environment.

In reviewing these findings, it is clear that the facts only partially support the theoretical framework. Authoritarianism is indeed related to career success in a bureaucratic setting. Political conservatism, which subsumes several values that seem functional in organizations, is similarly related. Finally insofar as alienation includes the rejection of organizational norms, highly successful executives rank significantly lower than their less successful brethren. However, this finding is strongly affected by class status: since the most successful executives tend mainly to come from upper-class backgrounds, they would be expected to rank lower on alienation.

Similarly, the most successful men do not defer to authority when this is quite specifically defined to mean their preferred relations with superiors and their acceptance of higher authority in matters closely related to their work. Indeed, contrary to one of our major assumptions, mobility is steadily and positively related to the desire for independence in both these areas. This is among our most significant findings and seems to merit considerable further research. The important thing, of course, is not whether this finding is consistent with our initial assumptions, but that individual attitudes toward authority are apparently a critical variable for differentiating those who work most effectively in a bureaucratic situation from those who are less effective.

Regarding the comparative findings, British managers seem significantly more liberal politically than the American group, but they are more alienated concerning the meaningfulness of human existence and the kinds of behavior required to get ahead. They are much less alienated, however, in their assumed ability to influence political affairs and in their opinion that government is effective in solving vital national and international problems. Finally, as a group, the British managers are much less inclined to accept the organization's influence in peripheral areas of work such as the use of the company's products and their off-the-job behavior.

Some Theoretical Implications

These findings have several implications for organizational theory and research. One concerns the origins of the values manifested by the members of an organization. This question in turn has implications for the scope of analysis required in organizational research. The data reported here suggest that the personal values governing behavior in the organization often stem from broad, cultural influences rather than (or in addition to) specifically *organizational* influences. The values that differentiate British and American executives seem less the product of the bureaucratic situation per se than of pre-organizational socialization, which in turn reflects class status. This is not new, since as Weber showed so clearly, the " pre-capitalist " religious values of certain Protestant sects proved of great utility in meeting the needs of a rational, disciplined industrial bureaucracy.[10] Yet, such events suggest that organizational research must be guided by a broad conceptual design that includes the total social system, insofar as its values seem directly relevant to organizational behavior. If, for example, executives in both private and public organizations in Britain are significantly more " pro-government " and politically liberal than their American counterparts, it seems that we must look to national cultural differences for the explanation, rather than to factors within the organization itself. Perhaps it is important to add, however, that even though such values are not organizationally determined, they affect behavior in the organization, and are consequently essential subjects for research.

In the same context, our research suggests that social class provides a more parsimonious explanation of high career mobility than attitudes toward authority. Certain attitudes toward authority are indeed associated with high mobility in the organization, but these attitudes may be essentially an intervening variable between class and job success. If this is so, it may be more economical to go directly to class as an explanatory variable, since among other advantages, it is easier to measure and is well established as a useful analytical construct. In this way, attitudes toward authority could be conceived as an example of the elements within the class rubric which have most relevance for organizational analysis. But the main point here is the apparent need to use a contextual approach in organizational analysis.

To some extent, our initial formulations accommodate such an approach. Following Sullivan, we assumed that reactions to authority are in part the result of experiences beginning in childhood, with the development of the " self-system " or personality. We noted that the way such attitudes are expressed in an organizational context is greatly influenced by the varying child-raising practices of middle-class and lower-class parents. Such formulations suggest that research on individual behavior in organizations must proceed at three interrelated but conceptually distinct levels: those of society, the organization, and individual personality. One resists this conclusion because it inhibits the tendency of behavioral research to focus on very small bits of reality. To some extent, it also undercuts the suggestive theory that the organization's own system of authority and values is the independent variable in personal accommodation. The work organization in effect becomes merely one among several instruments of socialization. Its major values are typically provided ready-made, so to speak, and the organization's function becomes the important one of reinforcing them in order that it may survive and prosper. At the same time, there is undoubtedly some reciprocity going on, in the sense that organizations may generate new (or modify old) social values in the light of their own experience.

Finally, while organizational research necessarily fixes on a given unit, it seems that we must also build into the research design some concept of the " seamless web " among society, a given organization, and personality. Certain bench-mark social values may be posited as givens. Enough research has been done on national cultural differences in Western countries to obviate the need for the researcher to isolate such values. At the organizational level, perhaps some variant of the ideal-type model will often prove useful if the research is to be kept manageable. Within these contexts, the variables of personality and personal accommodation to the organization can perhaps be researched intensively.

5

The Uses of Behavioralism

IT MAY BE USEFUL TO REVIEW SOME IMPLI-
cations of these several adventures in behavioral research.
My own belief is that an increased use of behavioral theory
and methods is essential for the continuing intellectual
development of public administration. They are also well
suited to it. The size, scope, and continuity of governmental programs invite behavioral research. Large aggregates of data are available; change and innovation are
typical; the problems of attracting and motivating young
people provide a vast research resource; and subjects such
as comparative administration badly need systematic field
research. These conditions, moreover, make possible a
cumulative research approach which has not been characteristic of either political science or public administration. A great deal of excellent research has been done,
but much of it has been idiosyncratic and rarely guided
by explicit theoretical propositions about organizational
behavior.*

The conclusion that reality is infinitely disordered and

* I am referring here of course to middle-range, research-oriented
theory in contrast to normative, democratic theory concerned with
administrative responsibility, and the like.

changing is both a cause and effect of this orientation. Everything depends, we are told, on presumably unique circumstances, and intuition and wisdom are the main properties of administration defined as art. The truth is that the theoretical innocence of public administration comes mainly from its position midway between the academic and the practical worlds. Our desire to be "men of the world" and our acceptance of the anxious demands of our students for insight into this world have done much to inhibit the intellectual development of our field. The belief that there is little or no consistency in human behavior is a related cause, leading to a futile piling up of discrete studies. The only scientific justification for a case study, for example, is its contribution to generalizations, yet in public administration such studies have consciously emphasized the dissimilarities rather than the uniformities of administrative behavior, and have led to the conclusion that every decision is unique. Surely social science is too young for this conclusion.

It is clear instead that science necessarily assumes consistent relationships. The assumption of some order, even if unknown, in the social and physical universe is essential to behavioralism, as it is to all science. This assumption has helped us learn a good deal about social behavior, about regularities in human interaction. Within limits, we can say that certain patterns of voting, consuming, and choosing characterize human behavior. The stable links between class status and group participation, intensity of voting, political tolerance, and style of life are another example. Such generalizations were built on the assumption that reality is ordered and that careful theoretical and empirical research can find such regularities. This assumption permits the inductive inferences that inspire scientific progress. To insist that we already know or that we can't know means the end of science.

A behavioral role is not easy, as I have tried to show. Behavioralists are awkward types. They ask embarrassing questions. They try to suspend judgment. They qualify endlessly. They must often disenchant those who have made their research possible. They seem to deny the role of individual insight and discovery that is part of our mythology concerning the advancement of knowledge. Worse, they are always telling us things we already know. Yet, when all this has been said, behavioral theory and research will, I believe, contribute more and more to the study of administration.

Certainly the relevance of community power structure analysis for administration is clear. It enables us to trace the interactions between political and administrative power. The extent to which public administrators share in certain kinds of major decisions is demonstrated. We learn something about the impact of local government structure upon the decisional process. In Mayor King's Edgewood, for example, a commission form of government directly affected participation. As he put it, " I couldn't bring in a lot of outsiders on these [governmental] decisions because I had already appointed an official group to handle them." In Riverview, a strong-mayor system encouraged the widespread use of coalitions of just such outsiders. In the process the structure of power was shaped: governmental decisions in Edgewood were monopolized by political and administrative officials; in Riverview, they were shared between these groups and economic outsiders.

The shape and intensity of a community's political culture also affects the distribution of influence. In Riverview where the major parties, ethnic, and religious groups were evenly balanced and ideologically inspired, politics became more than "beanbag," in Mr. Dooley's famous words. Political leaders and their administrative aides dominated the power structure for a decade. In Edgewood, a traditional nonpartisan politics and a homogeneous ethnic structure dampened conflict and contributed to greater issue specialization and the dominance (although by a small margin) of economic leaders. The end of ideology, as it were, gave local decision making a community-welfare, nonpolitical orientation. The irony is that pluralism, defined as a reasonably high level of citizen and group participation in the five major decisions, was higher in Edgewood even though its political culture was less diverse, self-conscious, and lively.

Such evidence enables us to specify more precisely the conditions under which local government officials will play active roles. Certain public or governmental decisions, mainly those involving state and federal grants, tend to be monopolized by local politicos and their administrative assistants. This is unexceptionable, but it challenges the assumption that political leaders are often mere pawns of economic elites. On the other hand, decisions which are essentially private and community-sponsored tend to be dominated by local economic leaders whose financial skill and control of large organizational and financial resources project them into leading roles. There is usually some overlapping in these issues, but the bulk of participants falls into one or another of these categories.

My own conclusion is that public administrators in small communities such as Edgewood and Riverview typically lack the resources of power, social prestige, and income usually necessary for decisive leadership in major issues.[1] They may possess skill and interest and time, but these are less viable than the hard resources monopolized by local economic leaders and the power of office enjoyed by their political rivals. This seems true regardless of the type of community decision, which as we have seen, tends to determine the relative power and participation of politicians and their economic rivals. Perhaps the only exception is local city attorneys whose legal skill and political connections bring them into governmental types of decisions where they work closely with the mayors who appoint them.

In sum, the use of power structure analysis helps one specify more precisely the roles typically played by public administrators. Their power compared with other local groups can be determined. The kinds of issues which they and their political masters typically dominate can be seen. The effects of local government structure on their roles and those of other elites become clearer. Nor is this information merely a by-product of research focused on political power. As Kent Jennings has shown, the method is applicable to analysis in which administrative power is a central concern.[2]

More directly relevant to public administration is the combined use of support theory and power structure analysis to determine the effectiveness of an organization. Support or exchange theory is applicable to virtually any type of organization, since all of them need resources and their very existence is reasonably good evidence that they are performing a desired service. It is obvious that organizations require resources, markets, and clientele support. The conditions under which these may be best secured are less obvious. Exchange theory enables us to specify the kinds of support and sources required for organizational viability and to test operationally the extent to which each is being used.

Since the conditions of organizational survival and efficacy are among the main concerns of our discipline, theory that can comprehend them adds much to our armamentarium. We already use these kinds of constructs, but usually in an impressionistic way. Most of us know that the annual appropriation struggles of USIS and AID, contrasted, say, with Agriculture or Commerce, reflect the absence of articulate interest group support for these agencies. But we lack the empirical data necessary to systematize the generalization. Instruments such as sociometric analysis can help us get beyond the pregnant speculation to firmer generalizations. No one should be put off by the knowledge that he is borrowing instruments from other disciplines. Instead, we might well take as our model sociology which has effectively used survey research and theoretical models such as functionalism in many substantive areas. Perhaps the test should be whether a theory or a method is productive, not what its disciplinary origins are.

Turning from an organizational to an individual level of analysis, one can be less sure about the utility of the theory of personal accommodation used to guide the research on the values of British executives. Here we are dealing with highly generalized attributes of personality, and with certain values that seem functional in a bureaucratic situation. Although attitudes toward authority are probably a vital mediator of job success and performance, the nature and direction of the relationship remains unclear. We can say with some confidence that a positive association exists between the attributes commonly defined as authoritarian and mobility in large bureaucratic structures. But authoritarianism includes a whole battery of values, only some of which can be directly related to authority in an organizational context.

When we turn to more specific manifestations of authority, the assumed relationships become cloudy. Indeed, the findings indicate that high mobility is associated with considerable *independence* toward organizational authority, whether this concerns general " organization-man " expectations regarding off-the-job behavior, or desired authority relations with superiors. In both contexts, successful executives were significantly more likely to reject organizational authority and to desire independence insofar as their own work was concerned. This finding may reflect *post hoc* rationalizations whereby an executive who has arrived may stress independence because it is more satisfying to his personal image. He may be compensating for the extended period during which dependent behavior was required, before he achieved his present position of relative autonomy. But this is mere speculation. The data show that successful men desire independence, and we must for the present accept their verdict.

The important conclusion is that the role of authority in organizational relationships merits further research. We may have to abandon the assumption that a generalized deference to authority is a property of successful executives, but it seems useful to continue work on other facets of the authority-accommodation relationship. As current study on the administration of scientific research suggests, the authority-legitimation concept is a valuable construct for understanding the preferences of highly-trained professionals for certain kinds of supervision and certain types of rewards.

The research also suggests the importance of comparative analysis, not only within a country and between countries, but also between public and private organizations. The two British samples were quite similar along certain

TABLE 37   Comparative status of private and public executives on five properties

Property	Proportion ranking "high" BIL (214)	BEA (197)
University education	40%	21%
Anxiety	6	14
Job satisfaction	60	49
Alienation	33	24
Class status (upper and upper-middle)	46	15

basic value dimensions such as political liberalism and the acceptance of a positive role for government in economic affairs. They differed, however, regarding the important specific properties listed in Table 37.

In general the British Industrials' group is advantaged on most counts. They have more education, higher class status, more job satisfaction, and less anxiety. Only in terms of alienation are they disadvantaged. This difference, incidentally, is almost entirely the result of a very high rate of alienation among BIL's top mobility group. This finding is exceptional because alienation is typically low among upper-class groups such as this. Perhaps anti-government feelings, including some disenchantment about their ability to limit government intervention in the private sector of the economy, account for this finding. Since the explanation for the differences in anxiety between the two groups might reflect the significant educational differences between them, we tested for this but found no important relationship.

Comparative analysis is also useful in differentiating British managers from their American counterparts. Using one sample from our community power study and another from the American research cited on p. 115, we compared the groups on a number of conservatism, authoritarianism, and alienation items. The American group proved to be significantly more conservative about government's role and its own influence in political affairs. On alienation items other than those dealing specifically with politics, however, the British managers were more alienated. Finally, the American group was consistently more likely to score high on authoritarian items honoring obedience, discipline, and the perception of individuals as being either weak or strong.

The American sample of executives (N-391) was used for comparison only on the four-item test concerning the legitimacy of the organization's influence in such areas as the use of its products and its expectations regarding its members' social behavior. Although both groups ranked the items in the same order, American managers were considerably more inclined to accept the organization's influence in all four areas. Such findings suggest that our assumptions about the relationship between attitudes toward authority and success may be more germane to the American milieu than to the British.

One important result of this kind of research concerns individual satisfaction in work. When enough research has been done on the attitudinal properties that differentiate successful from less successful executives in the big organizations that provide the work-place for most of us, we should be able to guide people into fields for which they are best suited. Effective placement and such vital personal by-products as joy in work may then become more common. We should also be able to predict job success with a higher level of confidence than at present. There is of course a great deal of concern about the reliability and validity of all kinds of testing, yet we have the word of Carl Rogers that even today psychological tests which cover both attitudes and skills are much more accurate than the judgment of a trained clinician using extended interviews.[3]

One final by-product may be mentioned: perhaps the behavioral approach can spark a new interest among students in the field of public administration. As I have tried to show, behavioral theories and methods can be widely applied. The attempts to test theory and the emphasis on field research have a certain fascination. One feels that he is dealing with relevant questions on a first-hand basis. He may feel that large aggregates of data permit reasonably secure generalizations. In some limited sense, the utility of one's research is restricted only by his imagination, by his ability to place his findings into meaningful contexts. Such are among the exciting prospects that a wider use of the behavioral approach can bring to the study of public administration.

Notes

CHAPTER 1

[1] Pritchett's work includes: *The Roosevelt Court* (New York: Macmillan, 1948); *Civil Liberties and the Vinson Court* (Chicago: University of Chicago Press, 1954); *The Political Offender and the Warren Court* (Boston: Boston University Press, 1958). Schubert's books include: *The Presidency in the Courts* (Minneapolis: University of Minnesota Press, 1957); *Constitutional Politics* (New York: Holt, Rinehart and Winston, 1960); *Quantitative Analysis of Judicial Behavior* (Glencoe, Ill.: Free Press, 1959); *Judicial Decision-Making* (ed.) (Glencoe, Ill.: Free Press, 1963).

[2] "Science as a Vocation," in *From Max Weber: Essays in Sociology*, trans. and ed. by H. H. Gerth and C. Wright Mills (New York: Oxford University Press, 1946), p. 138.

[3] As Arthur Bentley says, "if such a word as 'stimulus,' 'conscious,' or 'unconscious,' or 'observable' or 'behavior' itself behaves in half a dozen different ways on as many pages, the case is set down as one of 'incoherence.'" *Behavior, Knowledge, Fact* (Bloomington, Ind.: Principia Press, 1935), p. 12.

[4] Cited in Hans Reichenbach, *The Rise of Scientific Philosophy* (Berkeley: University of California Press, 1954), p. 3.

[5] Peter F. Drucker, *The Future of Industrial Man* (New York: John Day Co., 1942), p. 25.

[6] George C. Homans, *The Human Group* (New York: Harcourt, Brace and World, 1950), p. 36.

[7] In this section I am relying on Robert K. Merton, "The Mosaic of the Behavioral Sciences," in Bernard Berelson (ed.), *The Behavioral Sciences Today* (New York: Basic Books, 1964).

[8] A useful exception is Alfred de Grazia, "Government in Behavioral Science: Some Critical Notes," 7 *American Behavioral Scientist* (May, 1964), pp. 25-31. One unhappy example of this influence at work is reported in my *The Organizational Society* (New York: Vintage Books, 1965), pp. 304-06.

[9] Reichenbach, pp. 80-82.

[10] *Ibid.*, pp. 117-18.

[11] An example concerning Cornell University is found in A. J. Vidich, Joseph Bensman, and M. R. Stein, *Reflections on Community Studies* (New York: Wiley, 1964), pp. 313-49.

[12] Angus Campbell, *et al.*, *The American Voter* (New York: Wiley, 1960), pp. 512-15.

CHAPTER 2

[1] R. S. and H. M. Lynd, *Middletown in Transition* (New York: Harcourt Brace and Co., 1937); W. L. Warner and P. S. Lunt, *The Social Life of a Modern Community* (New Haven: Yale University Press, 1941); Floyd Hunter, *Community Power Structure* (Chapel Hill: University of North Carolina Press, 1953).

[2] *Ibid.*

[3] Studies of Congress, of course, make it clear that social class is associated with political power. Among others, see D. F. Matthews, *U.S. Senators and Their World* (Chapel Hill: University of North Carolina Press, 1960). That "political influentials" enjoy class advantages is also shown in Paul F. Lazarsfeld, B. R. Berelson, and H. Gaudet, *The People's Choice* (New York: Duell, Sloan, and Pearce, 1944); Elihu Katz and Paul F. Lazarsfeld, *Personal Influence* (Glencoe, Ill.: Free Press, 1955); and V. O. Key, *Public Opinion and American Democracy* (New York: Knopf, 1961). Key notes that "upper-income and occupational groups . . . contribute disproportionately" to those persons highly active in politics (p. 541). He also reports a positive association between "sense of political efficacy" and education and occupation, which are the usual determinants of class status (pp. 327-28). Group membership, political participation, and knowledge of public issues have

similarly been found to be positively associated with class status.

[4] Robert A. Dahl, *Who Governs? Democracy and Power in an American City* (New Haven: Yale University Press, 1961).

[5] For example, regarding urban renewal in Newark, one observer maintains, "It would be wrong to conclude that civic leaders are dissatisfied with their present role in renewal politics. They do not stand at the center of renewal decision making, but there is no evidence to indicate that they want to." Harold Kaplan, *Urban Renewal Politics* (New York: Columbia University Press, 1963), p. 113. Again, in a survey of renewal in American cities, Reuel Hemdahl reports, "In 80 per cent of the thirty-five cities that replied to the questions concerning support and opposition to urban renewal, local government, or a member of such a unit, first advocated urban renewal. . . . It is to be expected that the Mayor, rather than the City Council, should take the initiative and assume leadership in urban renewal, as well as in other areas of municipal affairs." *Urban Renewal* (New York: Scarecrow Press, 1959), pp. 235-36. Notable exceptions occur, as in Pittsburgh, where renewal was initiated by the Allegheny Conference, "a group of men who see and think big and care a great deal about Pittsburgh [and] decided the time had come to put the same vision, energy, and talent into working for the good of the community that they poured into their regular jobs" (p. 239). The author adds, "The Allegheny Conference is a community power structure, that has within its orbit the financial strength, the skill, and the influence to gain community objectives" (p. 241).

[6] Robert Presthus, *Men at the Top: A Study in Community Power* (New York: Oxford University Press, 1964).

[7] A careful analysis of power structure in four cities found an overlap of over ninety per cent between the two instruments. R. E. Agger, Daniel Goldrich, and B. F. Swanson, *The Rulers and the Ruled* (New York: Wiley, 1964), p. 331.

[8] See Henry S. Kariel, *The Decline of American Pluralism* (Stanford: Stanford University Press, 1961), p. 180.

[9] The most comprehensive of these is C. R. Wright and H. H. Hyman, "Voluntary Association Memberships of American Adults," 23 *American Sociological Review* (June, 1958), pp. 284-94. The

authors found that forty-seven per cent of families and sixty-four per cent of individuals belonged to no organizations, p. 286.

[10] J. E. Horton and W. E. Thompson, " Powerlessness and Political Negativism," 47 *American Journal of Sociology* (March, 1962), pp. 485-93; A. L. Green, " A Signpost for Research on Fluoridation Conflicts: The Concept of Relative Deprivation," 17 *Journal of Social Issues* (1961), pp. 26-36.

CHAPTER 3

[1] For an analysis of support theory and citations of related theoretical work, see R. H. Elling and Sandor Halebsky, " Organizational Differentiation and Support: A Conceptual Framework," 6 *Administrative Science Quarterly* (September, 1961), pp. 185-209.

[2] *Reflections on Public Administration* (University, Ala., University of Alabama Press, 1947).

[3] The following material is from L. V. Blankenship, " Community Power Structure and Organizational Effectiveness," in *Men at the Top*, Chapter 11.

[4] At the social motivational level, I have tried to analyze the interrelationship between organizations (i. e., between their members) and their cultural environment in poorer countries; " Weberian v. Welfare Bureaucracy in Traditional Society," 6 *Administrative Science Quarterly* (June, 1961); and " The Social Bases of Bureaucratic Organization," 38 *Social Forces* (December, 1959).

[5] For example, Elihu Katz and Paul L. Lazarsfeld, *Personal Influence* (Glencoe, Ill.: Free Press, 1955).

[6] F. J. Roethlisberger and W. J. Dickson, *Management and the Worker* (Cambridge, Mass.: Harvard University Press, 1939).

CHAPTER 4

[1] For a detailed analysis, see my *The Organizational Society*. Recent field research tests some similar hypotheses in Burma, Khim

Maung Kyi, *Accommodation to Authority in a Transitional Culture* (unpublished doctoral dissertation, Cornell University, 1965). I am encouraged in this approach by recent comments of sociologist George C. Homans who says, "I must insist again on the kind of explanation this is. It is an explanation using psychological propositions . . . , psychological in that they are commonly stated and tested by psychologists and that they refer to the behavior of men and not to the conditions of equilibrium of societies or other social groups as such." Again, "I now suspect that . . . the only general propositions of sociology are in fact psychological." See "Bringing Men Back In," 29 *American Sociological Review* (December, 1964), p. 817.

² Daniel R. Miller and Guy E. Swanson, *The Changing American Parent* (New York: Wiley, 1951).

³ *Modern Conceptions of Psychiatry* (New York: Norton, 1950).

⁴ I have considered the implications of some of these traditional values for the effectiveness of the British administrative class in "Decline of the Generalist Myth," 24 *Public Administration Review* (December, 1964), pp. 211-16.

⁵ T. W. Adorno, *et al.*, *The Authoritarian Personality* (New York: Harper, 1950).

⁶ T. W. Costello, "An Analysis of Attitudes toward a Planned Merger," 8 *Administrative Science Quarterly* (September, 1963), pp. 235-49.

⁷ It is important to note, however, that typical group dynamics of shared norms, friendship, and the like, do not always apply when *authority* enters the situation. George C. Homans, *The Human Group* (New York: Harcourt, Brace and World, 1950), pp. 116-17.

⁸ Burleigh B. Gardner, "What Makes Successful and Unsuccessful Executives," 13 *Advanced Management*, pp. 116-25; W. Lloyd Warner, *American Life: Dream and Reality* (Chicago: University of Chicago Press, 1953), p. 188; William Henry, "The Business Executive: The Psychodynamics of a Social Role," 54 *American Journal of Sociology*, pp. 286-91.

⁹ Mabel Newcomer, *The Big Business Executive* (New York: Columbia University Press, 1955); also, W. L. Warner and J. C.

Abegglen, *Occupational Mobility in American Business and Industry* (Minneapolis: University of Minnesota Press, 1955).

[10] Max Weber, *The Protestant Ethic and the Spirit of Capitalism*, trans. Talcott Parsons (New York: Scribners, 1958), Chapters 4, 5.

CHAPTER 5

[1] As Kent Jennings found in his study of community influentials in Atlanta, public administrators are often considered both by themselves and others as employees of local government. As one of them said, " I could grab the ball and run with it. But sooner or later they would catch up with me." *Community Influentials* (New York: Free Press, 1964), p. 65. Compared with elected officials and those in top economic positions, such appointed activists tend to rank low on both the reputational and decisional scales.

[2] *Community Influentials* (New York: Free Press, 1964). Another study which puts behavioralism to the service of public administration is F. P. Kilpatrick, M. C. Cummings, Jr., and M. K. Jennings, *The Image of the Federal Service* (Washington: The Brookings Institution, 1964). See also Robert L. Peabody, *Organizational Authority: Relationships in Three Public Service Organizations* (New York: Atherton Press, 1964).

[3] *On Becoming a Person* (Boston: Houghton-Mifflin, 1961), p. 368.

Index